Just RESPECT

ASHLEY ALEXANDER SMITH

WESTBOW
PRESS®
A DIVISION OF THOMAS NELSON
& ZONDERVAN

Scripture taken from the King James Version of the Bible

• Scripture quotations marked RSV are taken from the Revised Standard Version of the Bible, copyright © 1946, 1952, 1971 by the Division of Christian Education of the National Council of the Churches of Christ in the USA. Used by permission.

WestBow Press books may be ordered through booksellers or by contacting:

WestBow Press
A Division of Thomas Nelson & Zondervan
1663 Liberty Drive
Bloomington, IN 47403
www.westbowpress.com
1 (866) 928-1240

Because of the dynamic nature of the Internet, any web addresses or links contained in this book may have changed since publication and may no longer be valid. The views expressed in this work are solely those of the author and do not necessarily reflect the views of the publisher, and the publisher hereby disclaims any responsibility for them.

Any people depicted in stock imagery provided by Getty Images are models, and such images are being used for illustrative purposes only. Certain stock imagery © Getty Images.

ISBN: 978-1-9736-4178-0 (sc)
ISBN: 978-1-9736-4180-3 (hc)
ISBN: 978-1-9736-4179-7 (e)

Library of Congress Control Number: 2018911827

Print information available on the last page.

WestBow Press rev. date: 10/03/2018

Contents

Preface and Acknowledgements

The contents of this book were not intended to be seen as typically autobiographical or the writer's recall and recording of what he chooses to make known of the story of his life from the dawn of self-consciousness to the time of submission for publication. Rather, it is an attempt by the author to share with readers a perspective on:

a) The evolution of a leader in the context of a particular sector of society that is typically colonial and in the process of becoming post-colonial, dependent and typically self-doubtful as a nation whose ethos has been shaped largely by a combination of political and cultural imperialism and 'missionary' Christianity.

b) The struggle for recognition on the part of members of the awakening minority, the politically disenfranchised and economically deprived majority.

c) The dawning of psycho-historical and socio-theological awareness among non-European and non-Euro-American leaders of the religious organizations and the consequent emergence of the movement towards the attainment of independence among the various religious organizations with ties to metropolitan centres, mostly Great Britain and North America.

As is usually the case with persons who are products of unhealthy psycho-political situations, it was from outside of the indigenous context that this writer acquired the perspective from which the assessment of the content is made. It was during a two (2) year period of graduate studies in theological institutions in America that my perception of the social reality of the Caribbean and the situation in the church and society, acquired the shape it has had for me, especially since the late Nineteen Sixties (1960's). It is for this reason that I am fiercely nationalistic and committed to the principle of the right to decide on the authenticity of what is deemed to be true, valuable and best for every individual in whatever the context in which she/he lives and makes decisions about anything at any time.

For the spiritual resources out of which this story is conceived and has taken shape, I owe a great debt of gratitude to a multiplicity of categories of persons with whom I have interacted the fourscore years of my earthly sojourn.

I have been fortunate with my family of origin, my parents Adassa and Herbert Smith, my two (2) grandmothers, Dorcas and Rebecca, the siblings who have predeceased me, Myrtle, Inez, David and Orval, those who are alive at the time of writing, Olga and Lewis, my maternal and paternal uncles and aunts and my many teachers who have always affirmed me in my view from where I see things now, balanced and mostly gracious, in praising and scolding me. All the plusses of my life must be attributed to their graciousness towards me.

What I have said about relatives is applicable to those who have taught me in formal settings from 'ABC' school to graduate level education, especially in Jamaica and North America. Since the early years of my early adulthood I have been fortunate in having a number of fellow learners and professional colleagues who have contributed in no small way to the development of my intellect and character. These persons have come from a multiplicity of countries, ethnic backgrounds, religious orientations and political traditions. My life experience therefore, has been greatly enriched by my interaction with them and the friendships I have shared with them.

I have been particularly fortunate as a teacher and those I have taught in personal settings, have ranged in age from infancy to early seventies (70's).

For my development as a pastor I am indebted to my teachers while I studied at St, Colmes Presbyterian College. These teachers were of Calabar and Caenwood Theological Colleges which in the mid-fifties, merged to become Union Theological Seminary which eventually became a part of the United Theological College of the West Indies. Presbyterian Ministers Clement Thomas and Alfred Henry did much to prepare me for pastoral ministry during my years of internship in the Lowe River and Retirement Charges of the then Presbyterian Church in Jamaica.

For whatever I have been seen to be as a preacher since the early sixties, I am grateful especially to the saintly Professor of Homiletics at Lancaster Theological Seminary, Alfred Sayers. As an administrator, I am indebted to Professor Alfred Bartholomew of Lancaster Seminary; Professor Arthur Adams of Princeton Theological Seminary. For my development as a theological educator in the sub-disciplines of Sociology of Religion, Theology and Personality; Religion and Society, Psychology and History and Contemporary Theologies, I am indebted to Professors Samuel Kinchloe of the Interdenominational Theological Centre; Seward Hillner, James Emerson and Charles West of Princeton Seminary, and Bela Vassady of Lancaster Seminary, respectively.

In respect of my skills in dealing with various forms of racism in church and society at large, I owe a great deal to the late Raymond Schember a Minister of the then Presbyterian Church in the USA, his friends the Revd. George McCredie and his wife Lois, also of the Presbyterian Church, USA; my many friends in the Presbyterian Church in Ireland, and my colleagues of the United Church in Canada.

More than any other ethnic or national group, it was the Irish who helped me to understand that racism was not peculiar to the relationship between Europeans and Blacks, but is also among whites of different ethnic backgrounds and nationalities, and religious backgrounds. Credit for what appears on the printed page over or under my name is due largely to my relationship with a number of colleagues, and students, but especially to former teachers, the Reverend John Poxon, a missionary, then Warden of Methodist students at Caenwood College, Jamaica, who taught me Advanced English in theological college and Professor Harry Richardson, founding President of the Interdenominational Theological Centre, Atlanta, Georgia. The latter, who after reading a paper I had written on emotional and Intellectual Readiness for Christian ministry, advised me to keep on writing and seek opportunities for getting my work published.

Like the well known exponent of Black American Liberation Theology, James Cone, I have come to see every sermon, every lecture and every article for publication, as something worthy of my best effort and this has paid good dividends not only for me but also the Church, to the service of which, everything of which I am capable, has been dedicated, since the event of my ordination to the Ministry of Word and Sacrament on the Seventeenth of May 1955.

No one person nor category of persons deserves more credit for participation in my development than the four (4) who make up my family of procreation, - my wife Winnifred, our daughters, Faith and Grace and our son Bertrand. Despite my short-comings as a husband and father, they have each in her/his peculiar way, been relentless and unstinting in their support, criticism and encouragement, over the last forty-eight (48) years.

Because of the freedom each member of the family enjoys within the context of our home, and their own sensitivity in respect of loyalty to truth and appreciation of the feelings and tastes within the spheres in which they relate to others, I have been helped by them immensely to grow into what I have become.

Ministers of Religion, like persons of other callings, do not easily find colleagues with whom they can be unreservedly open about their doubts and fears and feelings of disappointment, anger and disgust. For about sixty (60) years I have had a the good fortune of the close friendship with the Reverend Clement Gayle, Baptist

Minister and Church historian and colleague on the faculty of the United Theological College of the West Indies.

Since the early nineteen eighties when I became a member of the legendary 'Dam Crew' I have been fortunate to have as walking partners, United Church Ministers Oliver Daley; and Stotrell Lowe, Baptist Minister and Biblical Scholar Burchell Taylor and Roman Catholic Archbishop of Kingston, The most Reverend Donald Reece. These brothers, along with my other colleagues, graduate students at the United Theological College and my Inter-faith colleagues Professor Ajai Mansingh, stand out in my memory as major contributors to what I am or seem to be.

Throughout the years of my career as pastor and administrator, I have been fortunate to be the recipient of much love, care, understanding and expressions of admiration and gratitude, from parishioners and neighbours in the various communities in which I have lived and served. If I am anything beyond what is basically human, it is largely because of the responses of these persons since nineteen fifty (1950) when as a student for the Christian Ministry I began to serve as assistant to pastors. What these persons claim that they saw in me is no more than the product of their own loving responses to what God has graciously permitted me to be to them.

For the preparation of what I have written in my sometimes unreadable handwriting, I am indebted to my most consistent critic and mentor, my younger daughter Grace Edwina, who committed herself to the typing of my manuscript as her contribution to the project which she has seen as belonging to the whole family which at the time of writing, also included daughter-in-law Sharon and grandchildren Hannah and Johnathan.

I make this exposition available to those who will read it in the hope that most readers will not only find it useful but also be inspired by it, to do likewise with their own story, in the service of humankind, especially those who find it difficult to accept themselves in their entirety as the Creator sees and loves them.

About Ashley Alexander Smith

On the seventeenth of May 2005 the Reverend Ashley Smith celebrated the Fiftieth Anniversary of his ordination to the Christian Ministry within the tradition of the Presbyterian Church in Jamaica which is now part of the United Church in Jamaica and the Cayman Islands.

Ashley Smith has served the church and the people of the Caribbean in various capacities since his ordination over fifty years ago. For forty-one of the fifty-three years as an ordained servant of the church, he was in full-time pastoral work in rural, inner city and suburban congregations with churches located in the parishes of St. Elizabeth, Trelawny, Manchester, St. Ann, St. Catherine, St. Andrew and Kingston.

In his own denomination he has chaired all Synodical committees except Finance, prior to his taking leave to serve ecumenically in the area of Theological Education. In the period 1969 to 1980, Rev. Smith served for as many as four one year terms as Moderator of the United Church in Jamaica and Grand Cayman, a union church which came into being in 1965 bringing together the Congregational of Union of Jamaica and the Presbyterian Church in Jamaica and Grand Cayman. It was while serving as a Moderator of his own denomination that the Reverend Mr. Smith was elected President of the Jamaica Council of Churches (JCC), a position he held between 1969 and 1972. It was during his incumbency as President of the JCC that the Anglican Church in Jamaica was re-admitted to membership of the Council and the Roman Catholic Church became a member. As a representative of his denomination on the Council of Churches, he served on both the Church and Society and Faith and Order Commissions of the body, consecutively. A committed ecumenist, Ashley Smith was a member of a group of Caribbean international church leaders that made up the committee that prepared the Caribbean Churches for the inauguration of the Caribbean Conference of Churches which came to birth formally in Jamaica in 1973. He served as a member of the executive committee of the regional ecumenical body until the mid-nineteen eighties.

Rev. Smith's involvement in the ecumenical movement extended beyond the Caribbean geo-political region. In 1973 he served as Minister at large for three months with the Presbyterian Church in Ireland. In the period 1975 to 1992 he served as Ecumenical Pastor with the United Presbyterian Church in the U.S.A on the study of the US-Cuba Relations, and as part of a committee appointed by the Presbyterian Church, USA, to prepare a mission statement entitled 'Towards a Culturally Plural Church', addressing the issue of racial and ethnic divisiveness within the constituency of that North American denomination. He was part of the Mission to the U.S.A. project in 1992, which took him to Presbyterian congregations in the Presbytery including Houston, Texas. His commitment to Christian unity led him to accept an appointment as Interim Minister of the Presbyterian Church in Grenada in 1998, making him the first Afro-Caribbean person to serve that church in one hundred and sixty-seven years.

In 1987, during his incumbency as President of the United Theological College of the West Indies (UTCWI), Ashley Smith was one of the Theological Educators from India, Indonesia, the Philippines, Ghana and the Caribbean, invited by the British Council of Churches to visit Theological Colleges in Great Britain, observe approaches to ministerial training in that country and make recommendations to the Council for changes in the curriculum of those institutions for the preparation of persons for leadership of the church in contemporary Britain.

Rev. Smith's involvement in theological education as a teacher began in1981 when he accepted an invitation to become the first holder of a lectureship endowed by the Lutheran Church in America. In the period September 1981 to July 1990, he served as Lecturer, Deputy President and President consecutively, returning to pastoral work in August 1990. As a member of the faculty of the United Theological College of the West Indies, Rev. Smith taught courses in the areas of Religion and Society and Theology and Religion. He redesigned the course entitled Church and Development and designed courses in Contemporary Trends in Theology and Introduction to the study of Religion.

It was during his incumbency as President of the United Theological College, that-the University of the West Indies (UWI) approved the programme of studies leading to the award of Graduate Degrees in Theology. It was also under his stewardship that arrangements were concluded for the collaboration of the United Theological College of the West Indies and Columbia Theological Seminary in Decatur, Georgia, U.S.A. for a Doctor of Ministry degree for persons involved in pastoral leadership across the Caribbean region. The Doctor of Ministry programme has served the purpose of bringing together persons of varying traditions who would not normally be inclined to work together in the context of the Caribbean.

Rev. Smith has worked with most students pursuing graduate work in the area of Religion and Society from the inception of the Master of Arts and Master of Philosophy programmes of U.W.I.- U.T.C.W.I.

Rev. Smith's interest in the writing of the 'Theology from Below' has provided him with ample opportunity for development during his stint as the Editor for the regional publication, Caribbean Journal of Religious Studies (C.J.R.S).

In addition to his own articles authored in the C.J.R.S. he has published three volumes of papers in issues related to Theology and Society: **Presentation in Jamaica – a Challenge to the Established**

Churches in Society (1975)[1], Real Roots and Potted Plants (1984)[2], and Emerging from Innocence- Religion, Theology and Development (1991)[3].

For many years Rev. Smith served as a member of the Theological Committee of the Caribbean and North American Area Council of the World Alliance of Reformed Churches. At the present time he is a member of the managing committee of the St. Micheal's Centre for Caribbean Spirituality.

Ashley Smith's understanding of Ecumenism opens him to socio-theological relationships that transcend the boundaries of Christian theology and inter-church interaction. Since the mid-nineteen eighties he has been involved in the promotion of interfaith dialogue with representatives of religious traditions including Hinduism, Islam, Bahai, Judaism, Buddhism, Blue Star Jamaica. In his capacity as Chairman of the Inter-faith Fellowship of Jamaica, he has worked with Professor Ajai Mansingh, Secretary of the group, in the arranging of Inter-Faith events staged at the Chapel of Mona Campus of the University of the West Indies, Kings House, University of Technology and in other fora organized by the Inter-faith fellowship. For twelve years he has been involved in the examination of and revision of the syllabus for Religious Education, one of the subjects offered by the Caribbean Examination Council.

Ashley Smith served for many years as the United Church Chaplain on the Mona Campus on the University of the West Indies. In that capacity he has had much opportunity for witness as an ecumenical person as representative of the humanity for the age of 'a world without borders'.

Many older Jamaicans will remember Ashley Smith as a person who has firm convictions about the role of the Church in the creation

---

[1] Smith, A. (1975). Presentation in Jamaica – a Challenge to the Established Churches in Society. Mandeville, Jamaica. Eureka Press Limited
[2] Smith, A. (1984). Real Roots and Potted Plants. Mandeville, Jamaica. Eureka Press Limited
[3] Smith, A. (1991). Emerging from Innocence-Religion, Theology and Development. Mandeville, Jamaica. Eureka Press Limited

and sustenance of a society that is truly human and reflective of the Kingdom of God as portrayed in the teachings of Jesus especially in the Gospel of Matthew. It is in keeping with this perspective on Salvation and the vocation of the new person in Christ that he has felt challenged to work in socio-political and pastoral roles as are exemplified in his stint as Advisor to the late Prime Minister, Michael Manley, during the nineteen seventies, member and President of the Caribbean Federation for Mental Health, and since October 2004, as President of the Caribbean Federation for Mental Health for the next biennial. The Rev. Ashley Smith has been cited for long and distinguished service by a number of Religious and Civic organizations in Jamaica: the Jamaica Council of Churches, Girls' Brigade Jamaica, The Kiwanis Clubs of North St.Andrew, Kingston and New Kingston, and the Caribbean Federation for Mental Health.

In preparation for over fifty years of service as a servant-leader of the church Ashley Smith has been a student of the former Presbyterian Theological College (St.Colme's), the University of London (external), Lancaster Theological Seminary, Pennsylvania, Princeton Theological Seminary, New Jersey and the Inter-denominational Centre, Atlanta, Georgia. He spent a semester at Columbia Theological Seminary, Decatur, Georgia during which time he read Contemporary Theology and taught Caribbean Church History.

At the present time he teaches courses in African Retentions and African Religious Influences on the Caribbean in the undergraduate and graduate programmes, respectively, at the University of the West Indies and the United Theological College of the West Indies, and works with graduate students in the areas of Religion and Society and Contemporary Theologies. He also teaches in the Tertiary Education Programme of the United Church in Jamaica and the Cayman Islands, International University of the Caribbean (IUC), Faculty of Theology.

A Jamaican who never loses faith in the ability of the people of Jamaica to overcome obstacles to their development, Ashley Smith is convinced that the most formidable challenge to national development is in the area of family life. With this conviction he misses no opportunity to mentor children, young people and parents, with special reference to the sacred vocation of bringing children into the world and helping them to become productive and responsible citizens equipped with the capacity to function with optimum effectiveness in an increasingly complex world.

Married to Winifred, a former Principal of Camperdown High School, Ashley is the father of three (3) adult children, (Faith, Grace and Bertrand) who are making their own contributions as participants in the making of the world of the current age.

N.B. This Tribute is from a paper prepared by a group of exponents of Public Theology in 2006. This ecumenical group was made up of the following persons: Anna Perkins (Roman Catholic), Neville Callam, Karl Johnson, Burchell Taylor (Baptist), Ernle Gordon (Anglican), Wanyeford McFarlene, Byron Chambers (Methodist) Garnett Roper (Missionary Church in Jamaica), Roderick Hewitt, Majorie Lewis, Stotrell Lowe, Richmond Nelson, Ashley Smith (United Church in Jamaica and The Cayman Islands).

Just Respect!

While studying in the United States of America during the 1960's, I always had to explain to my hosts and classmates that my socio-economic background was rural, small farm lower middle class. In fact, I had great difficulty convincing fellow students that small farm in Jamaica meant not having enough land on which a tractor could operate and not more than a donkey or mule as the means of transporting what was produced on the small subsistence farm.

My host or colleagues almost invariably expressed doubt about my description of my background. They had great difficulty figuring out how someone with that sort of background could be so much at ease in situations like theirs in which most persons with whom I interfaced were the products of white, upper-middle class, urban, suburban or mid-town, growing up in homes with access to electricity and piped water and coming from homes where there was at least one car to a family, and if from rural areas, being used to seeing the farmer furnished with tractor and at least small motorized vehicle with which to transport the product of his farm which would be scores if not hundreds of acres in size.

My hosts, classmates and professors were even more skeptical of my account of life and training up to that point. When I told them that I had none of my training outside of Jamaica and most if not all in deep rural areas before my twenty-first birthday, I remember a professor telling me to my face that no one with my ethnic characteristics could have acquired the faculty I demonstrated

1

in the use of standard English, without being exposed to tertiary education in the United Kingdom or having grown up in an urban or suburban upper middle class home.

My fellow choristers in the Lancaster Seminary choir marveled at my familiarity with the music of white suburban or downtown upper middle class euro-American churches. Needless to say, they found it difficult to believe that in my own country there was no such thing as 'Black' Church or 'White' Church. Persons in the churches I attended wondered how I could be so much at ease in their midst when normally black and white persons did not mingle even in Christian worship in their part of the world. I remember the father of a member of a Presbyterian congregation of which I was supply pastor in the summer of 1961, insisting that I was not black since nothing about me fitted the picture he had in mind when he thought of someone who was 'dark' or 'Black'. Incidentally, that brother designated me 'British'. Of course, he would have been more concerned about explaining to his neighbors how I came to be a guest and pastor of his daughter, son-in-law and grandchildren.

All that I have said in the foregoing paragraph, in an attempt at offering an interpretation of my becoming, who, how, and what I am, and why some whose origins are identical end-up not only being disappointed with themselves but blaming any number of factors and categories of persons for what they fail to become or achieve.

I attribute all the positive things about myself to one thing above everything else, RESPECT. I am what I am because throughout my life I have received respect from significant persons in all the spheres in which I have interacted with persons. This does not mean that I have always enjoyed the good will and support of everyone. What it means is that I have always had the feeling of being affirmed or taken seriously, by those whose view of me mattered to me. What is most interesting about being respected is that those who show respect for you also expect much of you and would even help to ensure that their expectations are not misplaced.

I am convinced that my siblings have been of the view that my parents expected more of me than of them, and in keeping with their expectations, did more for me in a number of subtle ways which children are quite capable of discerning, and even scolded me less severely even when the offence committed by me would have been more serious than those committed by them.

With my teachers, the respect accorded me was more obvious. Some appeared to have been quite naïve about the ability of their pupils and their parents to detect bias in favor of some pupils who were preferred for one reason or another. What is well known is that in many cases pupils are favored because of what they present of themselves, and are given preferential treatment because those who are favoured tend to become more favorable and vice versa. This indeed is what is implied in the statement attributed to Jesus in the Parable of the Talents recorded in the Gospel according to Matthew (Chapter 18 vs. 29, 30), "To everyone who has will be given, and he will have abundance, but from him who has not, even what he has will be taken away". (RSV)

In my case, because of the respect I got from parents, uncles, aunts, grandparents, adult members of the community, significant visitors to home, school, church and community, I very early internalized the attitude of these significant persons towards me, became self-respectful very early in my development, and with the help of insights gained from the study of social and developmental psychology, became convinced that respect from others engenders and reinforces self-respect in persons and self-respect engenders self-confidence, respect for others engenders and reinforces self-respect in persons and self-respect engenders self-confidence, respect for others, faith in God and in others, and hope.

What is most important to me about respect is what my own experience has helped me to discover about some of the social problems of my own country and countries with a similar history and psycho-historical background. It is that most of the social problems related especially to the behavior of boys and young men of what some refer to as the 'underclass', stem from the fact that those who underachieve, misbehave and get involved in crime, are invariably those who have received little or no respect from any category of persons. Our children with behavior problems are all persons who have not been consistently loved at home, in the neighborhood, at school, or anywhere else. As a consequence of not being properly loved or loved with respect, they have not seen the need to please or reward anyone by way of face to face respectful response, effort towards personal achievement, or even behavior change in the hope of earning social credit not hitherto accumulated.

Someone who had a satisfying career in education told me of the case of a young man who ended up at school in which she taught after being asked previously to leave two schools. Of the five subjects taken by him in the secondary school examinations he failed four and obtained a distinction in one. When asked how he came to do so badly in so many and so well in the one in which so many tend to do so badly, his reply was eye opening. He said that he did so well at the subject he passed because the person who taught that subject was the only teacher from whom he got respect. Therefore he did as well as he did in the subject in response to the respect she gave him. Two things about that story however are that it was not given the publicity it deserves and even those who have heard it would not necessarily have seen the importance of the lessons for teachers. Indeed there are too many cases in which what is lacking at home is compensated for at school, but equally true is the tragic fact that in most cases that which is lacking at home is complemented and reinforced by what happens at school. This, more than anything else, explains the proliferation of the cases of young persons who are not only failing at school but also becoming failures in the school system and thereby threatening the safety of the rest of society even before the end of their days at school.

Unfortunately, in societies like that of Jamaica, institutions like the Christian church do not make much difference because they reflect too much of the attitudinal defects in society that contribute to the prevalence of disrespect which is the single most significant cause of delinquency, under-achievement at school, anti-social behavior and worst of all, criminal activity on the part of those who are deprived of healthy parental love and subject to disrespect from those from whom they expect genuine appreciation.

With respect to parental love, it is very necessary to emphasize that children of parents who are materially better off do not necessarily fare better than their counterparts whose parents lack the means of providing for their basic material needs. It is known that many children are pampered with things by parents who are secretly hateful of their children for one reason or another, and therefore, use material gifts as substitutes for genuine parental love. Many of such parents see their children as obstacles to their personal advancement socially and at the work place. There are others who see in their children traits or physical features which they detest in their parents, their spouses or parents of spouses whom they resent, very often, unconsciously. Not infrequently children are resented, and correspondingly disrespected, because significant persons in their spheres of reference are unhappy with their physical characteristics, academic progress, speech patterns, choice of friends and even career choice. It is not uncommon for children to detect resentment of themselves in their parents. Some even overhear negative comments by parents on features of themselves. Needless to say, what is true of parents is also true of siblings, teachers and other significant personages.

Those who happen to be part of the so-called under-class are likely to be victims of multiple disrespect which is very often not even subtle. Some are told very crudely and openly about being 'ugly', 'dunce', 'good for nothing' and 'not likely to come to anything'. Not infrequently they are snubbed by teachers and schoolmates and ignored in public areas, because of inelegance in speech, personal appearance and lack of poise, the last being a consequence of a combination of a number of all of the others.

What is most disturbing to me as a student of Christian ethics and leader in the Christian community is that much of what is alluded to in the foregoing paragraphs is no less true among Christians than it is among those who may even be indifferent to preachings or claims of Christians. Those who attend schools sponsored by churches, belong to 'Christian' homes and work for 'Christian' bosses and with Christians at the workplace, tell stories about the experience of disrespect that are very similar to those told by their counterparts in places where religion is never mentioned by those who call the tune or make the important decisions. In fact, in many cases some who are Christians are even more likely to be disrespectful and discriminating especially when dealing with the uninitiated.

Where the approach to children is concerned, what is true of Christian parents is that despite what they say to their children verbally about the teachings of Christ, many children of Christian parents end up with the same negative approach to themselves as their peers whose parents' approach to religion is less formal and certainly less open.

My own experience from childhood has served to strengthen my conviction that assurance of respect from others reinforces self-respect in the recipients of respect. In fact, it not only makes the recipient respectful of himself/herself, it also predisposes him/her to be respectful of others and as a consequence, more likely to be affirmative of others, patient with them, supportive of their efforts to make something of themselves and willing to work with them rather than against them or in competition with them.

Respect, which is a vital component of disinterested or 'neighbor-regarding' love, is the most valuable human resource. Its value is not only spiritual but also social and economic. Assurance of respect, especially from significant others, empowers persons and those who feel empowered are, first of all, free to be respectful of others. Those who do not have to be preoccupied with getting respect have the inner resources that render them optimally productive, resourceful, courageous, persevering, and forgiving towards others and self, and hopeful.

The vast resources in respect of time, money and skills, now being expended on security and diplomacy at local, national and international levels, would be available for the meeting of the basic needs of poverty-stricken people of our world, if those who now claim to be enlightened would just show some more respect, first to persons of their own household, and then, to all others not because they are deserving, but just because they are human. Needless to say, those who are humanized through the experience of being respected are likely to be led to discover and appreciate their own worth in the presence of God whose love for all creation is totally unconditional and boundless.

The Blessings of Demanding Parents and Teachers

Nothing is more detestable to adolescents and young adults than parents and teachers who demand perfection in all things. Of course, everything these adults demand is good for these younger people, however difficult or unnecessary it may seem to those who have to meet the expectations of others.

One of the parental demands on my siblings and me was getting out of bed before half-past four every weekday morning in order to go about three miles from home to get the cows and milk them; we had to "tie them out" where they could get fresh grass and water during the day until it was time for them to be moved to where they could be as secure as possible. It seemed cruel then, but I recognized the value of this rigor when I found myself with the habit of rising early in college and getting some work done when others in my flat or dormitory were fast asleep. I attribute much of the success I have had in life to the discipline of getting out of bed before five in the morning, wherever I am, and getting writing done or getting ready for the early morning walk with my friends. I was instilled with the discipline to get the best grade possible, and I attribute this discipline to the pressure put on me, especially by my father, to stay at the top of the class at all times.

Consistency in the achievement of excellence is something that every self-respecting person cherishes, and this comes not as much from natural ability or self-motivation as it does from the fear in early life of disappointing those who expect only the best from you.

Children achieve academically and behave exemplarily not so much out of the instinctive urge to outperform their peers as out of the need to reward those significant persons in their spheres of reference who they perceive to be expecting much of them. Whenever I undertook any task as a child or adolescent, a number of persons came to mind.

These included my parents, Miss Dine (the lady who ran the ABC or infant school where I learned the basics of reading, writing, and numbers), my class teachers at the Blauwearie Elementary School, and a number of persons who continually expressed admiration for me and the wish to see me do my best. I was compelled to retain their high expectations. It worked for me (to the disgust of those who expected to get ahead of me even occasionally).

The school principal and my parents were disappointed with me on one occasion when I went along with some other boys beyond the destination to which we were sent by the principal. The other offending members of the truant group were excused; I was severely rebuked because everyone expected more from me. I have never forgotten the pain I felt on hearing those stinging words of rebuke. It left me with no doubt that I was destined for leadership. That message was not wasted on me. Throughout my life I had never had to lobby for an appointment. I have always been offered opportunities to lead, persuaded to accept these positions, and assured of the support of those requesting that I assume leadership.

My father, a small farmer, was unusually insightful for a person in his position. A very proud person, he was for me a resident tutor in black nationalism. He was full of resentment for racial discrimination in the world and for color prejudice in his immediate social environment. Very few of his peers comprehended what he stood for or what he said. Many saw him as being in the wrong place and out of his league.

He was often ridiculed for what he said about the need for education up to the highest level for black Jamaicans of his time. Many were of the view that pursing education could be a waste of time and money, since there would be no chance of black persons of small towns, urban ghettos, or rural areas getting employed in areas then reserved for whites, high browns, and mulattoes. What happened to his own children and many of their contemporaries has proved him right and his critics wrong.

Corpy, as he was known, spent much of his meager earnings on books of a variety of subjects. It was from one of his books entitled *The Progress of a Race* that I got my first insights into the nature and evil effects of American racism, especially as it applied to the descendants from black African enslaved people who, like their counterparts in the Caribbean, were both the chief instruments for the accumulation of American capital and economic power and the worst victims of Western civilization.

A keen student of the teachings of Marcus Garvey, my father was convinced that the socioeconomic and political structure of his day was not only evil and contrary to the will of God, but also destructible and replaceable. His understanding of history and of the central message of the Bible led him to believe that what obtained was contrary to the will of God and could be brought to an end by God through the instrumentality of persons motivated by faith in the God of the people of Israel, of Jesus the Christ, and of all those whose names have been associated with the defiance and persistence in historical events like the abolition of slavery, the Morant Bay rebellion, and other special epochal events—especially in the histories of oppressed people like Afro-Caribbeans and Afro-Americans. Wherever he had an audience, especially in the company of men and boys, he told stories of overcomers in the biblical history, English history, and the history of North America and Jamaica. Those stories were told in the walks to the field, over dominos and card tables, at church, and before we (his children) fell asleep at nights.

Unlike a lot of other reluctant colonial subjects, however, he saw possibilities for ending inequities mostly in a logical, meaningful formal education and a national approach to the religion of the day. Without ever hearing a word of what liberation theologians refer to as a hermeneutic of suspicion, he insisted that we read between the lines, especially what was written or said by those who enjoyed unfair advantages locally and at the global centers of power. As far as he was concerned, there could be no change in the status quo politically and economically without education of the disadvantaged. This is why he was prepared to put every penny he could find in books and private tuition not only for his sons but also for his daughters. He preached the gospel of higher education not only in conversations with his fellow small farmers, but at parent-teacher meetings and the meetings of the local branch of the farmer's agricultural society.

My father saw education as a political tool, and he saw politics as a feature of every facet of life, including religion. Again, this is why he spent money on books, read the books he owned, and insisted that his children read everything they could find, anywhere.

Our parents were among the few of the village who bought the available newspaper, *The Gleaner*. Of course, the paper was bought only on Saturdays, but occasionally a copy was at the shop at the square; since he was considered one of the better readers, it was usually he who read the latest news and led the discussion on the contents. He never failed to relay the latest news to us when he came home.

Although very few persons around town, other than the teachers, spoke Standard English, my father insisted that only Standard English should be spoken in any conversation. Of course he was overheard speaking patois with his friends.

My parents were ardent members of their respective churches; my mother was Presbyterian, and my father was Baptist. As children we had to attend the Presbyterian Sunday school because this was where most of the weekday school teachers taught, and the principal of the school preached on most Sundays, in the absence of the minister who preached on only one Sunday per month when he came to administer the sacrament of the Lord's Supper or to perform a baptism.

I often went to the Baptist church when the minister preached or when there was a special occasion on which a number of visiting ministers shared the platform with the minister in charge. Among the Baptist ministers I knew in early life was one named O. T. Johnson and another named Clarence Whylie. They were both men of stature who made good impressions on me. The Presbyterian minister of my youth and young adulthood was the Reverend John Wint, father of the famous athlete Arthur Wint; his brothers were Lloyd and Douglas, and his sisters were Mavis Edwards and Kathleen Edwards. My father spoke highly of these preachers largely because they seemed always well prepared and respectful of the local people. He detested all speakers from pulpits and elsewhere who appeared to be taking their audience for granted.

My father was keen on the boys in his home "keeping themselves to themselves" as far as relationships with women were concerned. Somehow or another, out of his more discerning knowledge of the dynamics of the local community, he felt that young men who were keen on getting ahead were always vulnerable to the designs of young ladies and their mothers. I grew up to understand the reason for his fears. Fortunately for me, I heeded his advice and remained grateful to him and others of his ilk. There is nothing more desirable for a man than to have all members of his family under one roof.

My father always pointed to his father as an example of the dangers of loved ones having more than one family. Needless to say, the fact that his undesirable situation is so common does not make it less acceptable for any person, community, or nation.

Despite his commitment to the observance of moral principles based on the ethics of the Christian Church, the last thing he wanted to hear was that any of his children would follow a career in the Christian Ministry. One of his heroes as a son of the Parish of Hanover was the celebrated Jamaican advocate and legislator J.A.G. Smith. The frequency with which he spoke of that distinguished Jamaican, left me in no doubt whatever that he would have been delighted if I saw him as a professional role model and prepared myself to follow in the footsteps of this great Jamaican of pre-independence Jamaica. When I announced to him that I was persuaded that a career in the Christian ministry was God's will for me, he was visibly disappointed and responded verbally by asking me to think it over for a year. At the end of the year of contemplation when I told him that my conviction remained the same, he assured me that he would give me whatever help he could and pray that I would be a faithful servant of God. He kept his word until his passing nearly forty years after. My father's fears about my becoming a Minister of the gospel had nothing to do with the fact that the churches make so little provision for the support of their fulltime servants, but rather that many of the Ministers he knew, fell so short of his ideal of the Christian Minister. He actually named a person he would not want me to emulate. Much of what I have become must be credited to the determination of my part not to let down those like my parents, my teachers and the Ministers immediately responsible for mentoring me as a person, a discipline of the teachings of Christ and a servant of the people.

Among the things I learned from my mother, were the needs to remain financially independent, morally upright, worthy of a woman she would be pleased to have as a daughter in law. When the 'old man' was hard put to find the money for tuition fees, books, clothes and pocket money, she was always amused and ready to pull out some old 'notes' from one of her places where she hid them from the men in the house. She was always insistent that we do not spend as much as we earned and that we lend if we had to in order to help someone, but never borrow from anyone. For mother, living within one's means was one sure way of achieving personal independence and earning respect. Always skeptical of those who sought loans from her or father, she saved the 'old man' from the consequences of being too quick to lend his savings to anyone who came with a 'hard luck' story. Father and mother were a good match for each other, the one reserved and overcautious, the other outgoing, talkative and intellectually adventurous. They were good role models, not only for their children, but also for most of the people in the neighborhood. The old man went in his eighty-eighth year, and the old lady, in her ninety-second. They certainly deserved their rest and the place they hold in the memory of children, relatives and the rest of the local and wider communities.

'Chosen' or 'Called' for Ministry

Despite all that I have been persuaded to believe about 'call' in respect of the decision to pursue full-time work in the Church as a pastor, pastoral administrator and preacher after over 50 years since I was approved by the former Presbyterian Church in Jamaica in 1949, I am still of the view that in my case, it was choice by God in collaboration with persons other than my parents or myself.

As mentioned elsewhere, it was the wish of my nationalistic father that I pursue a career in law, with the renowned J.A.G. Smith as my role model. The great jurist and legislator was not only black but also from the Parish of Hanover, not many miles from where my 'old man' grew up. Of course, without the usual basic educational foundation provided by the traditional grammar schools of the pre-Norman Manley era of Jamaican politics I would have to get into legal studies by the route of the matriculation examination made accessible to persons outside of Great Britain by the University of London. I planned to get there by way of teaching. So I taught at the Williamsfield Primary School in Westmoreland for three years during which time I had pupils such as Minister of Agriculture of the late 90's and early 2000's, Roger Clarke.

Something happened on the late afternoon of the annual agricultural show on the Frome Sugar estate's show grounds, 1948. As I was standing alone reflecting on some of the things I had seen during the day, the Rev. John Wint, my mother's pastor came along and engaged me in conversation about my future. Among the things he said to me was that he was aware that I was trying to make up my mind about what to do in life from there on. Before I could complete a sentence in response, with the typical John Wint smile on his face, he said "I have been observing you for a long time and praying for you. I am convinced that you are the type of young man we are looking for in the service of the Church. Think about it and talk with me again when you think you need some help in making up your mind".

When I spoke to my father about what the Rev. Wint had said to me, his immediate response was: "I can't make up your mind for you but I can tell you that I would not be too happy about that. I am not so happy about some of those Ministers. However, give yourself about a year before you make up your mind". Of course, at that time he was a deacon at the Baptist Church, the Minister of which was the Rev. Clarence Whylie whose church I attended most Sundays while I stayed in Williamsfield where I was teaching in the primary school.

When after a year I told my father that I was convinced that the Christian Ministry was where God wanted me to serve, his reply was that he would give me as much help as he could and would pray that I become a faithful man of God and not like some he had known.

Interestingly enough, during the years of my training he became a member of the Presbyterian Church in which he was made an elder and was even selected to represent the church at Synod during the late fifties.

My call to ministry has been both challenged and tested ever since the afternoon when I was confronted by my mentor. The late great John Samuel Wint was to play a significant role in my formation as a theological student, pastor and leader in the Church. In many cases those who challenge, express disappointment that I did not follow a calling in which I might have been more directly involved in the struggle for political and social liberation. Students of the history of the Europeanisation of the Caribbean, insist that the so-called mainline Christian churches are instruments of colonial domination and by extension, a party to the suppression and depoliticisation of people of colour all over the world and especially in the Caribbean. Needless to say, I have lived with that conviction but long been convinced of the possibility of using my opportunities in the church, of subverting these structures of domination. After nearly sixty years since I was asked to contemplate the possibility of serving God and the world in the capacity of a Christian Minister, I am fully assured that I did the right thing, and further, that like Jeremiah I was chosen by God before I made the choice in response to promptings by my mentor John Wint.

I have come to my conclusion about the appropriateness of my choice of vocation not only on the basis of what European and North America theologians have written about the Christian concept of call, but rather, on the basis of my own understanding of what is behind the word 'GOD' as used in our culture and the role of the prophet in Jewish and other traditions. I am convinced that despite my shortcomings and failings the purpose of my 'call' has been fulfilled in large measure in the course of my life, especially since the beginning of formal training for work as a servant-leader under the aegis of the Christian church.

Despite what would seem to many as my preoccupation with issues of ethnicity, and justice for blacks and other categories of victims of injustice in the name of church, state, class or gender, my call and the work that I have been privileged to do, have reference not to any particular race, Christian tradition or religion, or nation, but indeed, to all of humankind. The practice of ministry has led me into interaction with fellow human beings of all continents and all social types. In the course of my ministry I have collaborated with Americans, Africans, Australians, Canadians, Chinese, Japanese, Koreans, Samoans, British (of England, Ireland, Wales and Scotland) and people of all language groups of the Caribbean. One of the discoveries that I have made is that in the final analysis, it is our humanity that matters most not our racial identity, nationality, religion, gender, medical condition or age. My interaction with my brothers and sisters of the various nationalities has led me to the conclusion that the call to service in any career is a call to work with God in what God is doing to set human beings and other areas of God's creation free to achieve maximum fulfillment in history.

In short, as one called of God my obligation to the enslaved in Eastern Europe, India or North America is no less than the one to the oppressed in Southern or Western Africa and in the Caribbean. The context of enslavement may differ but the objective of efforts at liberation is the same in the light of my understanding of God and the mission of Christ to which my call is related. By the same token, it is my view that enslavement in the context of any form of religion is obstructive to the process of creation, as political, social, and economic enslavement, according to my own theology. Therefore there can be no distinction between what I do in Evangelism in the context of the church and what I do in politics in the context of my country of citizenship. I get this from my reading of the Jewish prophets and the record of life and the ministry of Jesus the Christ who lived his early life in the context of political, religious and social milieu of a small town in the Middle East. My call was a call to minister in God's world in relation to every aspect of life in God's world. Needless to say, this call comes to every human being in some form or another and it is no less valid when it is not interpreted in relation to what, in my case, I refer to as the Christian Ministry. My father's call to farming and village leadership was no less valid than mine. So is my mother's call to mothering, my wife's call to teaching in the formal school system of the nation, and for that matter, the call of anyone else, to make his/her contribution to the making of the world. One of the regrettable things about the language of the institutionalized church is the tradition of assigning a higher value to the work of the 'ordained' person and using the words 'call' and 'calling' only of the vocation of the priest or Minister.

The traditional view of vocation within the Christian community and throughout the history of organized religion, has led not only to the undervaluing of the contribution of persons to the common good but also to the persistence among Christians of the view that those designated 'pastor', 'priest' or Minister in the Christian community should be only marginally involved in the cut and thrust of the life of the local community or nation. So many Christians view with suspicion the open involvement of religious leaders in elective politics.

They hold the view that one cannot be faithful to one's 'call' to preach and give pastoral leadership while being seriously involved in political leadership at any level. In the context of Jamaica this is rather interesting since so many of the pioneers in the making of the nation's political history have been leaders of the Christian church, lay and ordained. As many as three of those designated 'National Hero' were deacons of the pre- emancipation and immediate post-emancipation periods of the nation's history. Again, it is on record that among the founding members of one of our political parties were two ordained clergymen of the Anglican and Methodist churches.

In the tradition of the prophets of the Old Testament I have seen my own call to ministry as a challenge to give leadership to the community in its entirety and not just to the small segment of it referred to as 'church', 'denomination' or 'congregation'. The notion of the sovereignty of God over all creation is incompatible with that of a God whose concern is limited to 'spiritual' transformation of persons and with only that segment of humanity that is deemed to be the community of those referred to as "faithful".

In my own view, my call has reference to everyone and everything that falls under the sovereignty of God. This is why I feel no compunction about reaching out to all human beings, not just across Christian denominations, but indeed across all religious and ideological divides. Needless to say, this explains my commitment to ecumenical and interfaith relationships. It is also the reason I have always seen evangelization in terms of setting persons free to affirm the world which is the object of God's love and enabling those who are free to 'grow into the fullness of the stature of Christ', to become truly human in the sense in which creation of humankind is referred to in the first chapter of the book of Genesis. It is in this view that I speak without reservation, not only of theologies of liberation but also of theology as an instrument of liberation, the sense in which Jesus perceived it, as reported in the eighteenth verse of the second chapter of the Gospel according to Luke.

Making a Leader of a Country Boy

The making of a leader anywhere, is the work of God through large numbers of persons. It has been no different in the case of the son of 'Miss Das' and 'Corpy' and grandson of "Miss Darky", "Miss Becki" and "Maas Bob". Of all the men that exercised authority over me, my father, Herbert William Smith has been, by far, the most significant. However very significant also was my pastor of many years, the Rev. John Samuel Wint, Presbyterian Minister in the Brownsville Charge which spanned villages in Eastern Hanover and North Western Westmoreland. Teachers R. S. Robinson and R. G. Dinham, my uncle, Douglas McKitty and to some extent, the Rev. Clarence Whylie of the Baptist Church of which my father was a member for most of his life.

In addition to my mother who taught me to be independent on matters related to money and favours, women who influenced me greatly were Miss "Dine" McKenzie my 'ABC School' teacher, Mrs. Hilda Wint, the wife of the Rev. John Wint, my father's cousins "Aunti T" (Munroe) and Aunt Vin (Harrison).

All of the persons named, in one way or another, made it difficult for me to fail at anything that has gone into the making of my character. The people in all the villages in the broad area within which I interacted with persons, treated me as if I were answerable to all of them for whatever I was or did and they were responsible for ensuring that I fulfilled what in their view was my destiny. Needless to say, that destiny had to do with the achievement of excellence in whatever I attempted to do and the maintenance of blamelessness in moral character. Of course, I was just one of the many young persons who enjoyed that privilege. Needless to say, there were some of whom nothing was expected and of whom nothing was thought. And what each became was almost invariably according to the expectations and wishes of the people. It is as if the young are willed into what they eventually became.

There was something that teachers were and did that motivated and inspired the ambitious youth. Led by the Principal who was always a 'man-teacher', teachers seemed always well prepared for the classroom, keen on ensuring that their pupils learned all that was taught so that they could become at least, no less knowledgeable than their mentors were. Teachers dressed neatly, spoke 'properly' and appeared to behave as well as they insisted that their pupils behaved-impeccably! Of course, occasionally we learned that what we saw was what they were careful to allow us to see of them. They were careful to keep their unseemly behavior hidden from their credulous observers.

In those days who taught you and thought well of you followed your career as long as they were able to keep track of you. I remember, when I was well in my thirties, hearing elderly persons of my community of origin say "Im grow big eh, im all married", "Im turn out well and 'im 'mannersable' same way".

All of the foregoing just explains that notion that those who make it in the rural area are invariably those who are brought up not by their parents but by the entire village – neighbours, shopkeepers, police persons, watchman, teachers, lay preachers and the parson who visits once monthly to preach at communion service and occasionally to make house visits when someone in the village in seriously ill, or has done something to bring shame on an upstanding family or the church.

Young men and women who were expected to go far and 'carry off' their parents, the school and the community, were expected to stay away from questionable places like bars or where the men 'threw the dice', and avoid speaking 'patois' or 'bad grammar'. Good behavior and 'proper' speech were always the hallmark of the identity of those who were expected to do well in life. Unfortunately, this was not expected of everyone. There were some who were always free to behave anyhow, speak anyhow and not get very far. The makers of the leaders were always very selective and sometimes cruel. It was important for you not to 'let their bad mouth catch you'.

Those who were making it did not always enjoy the goodwill of everyone. There were those who expected you to go so far and no further. There were others who were fearful that if you did too well the bad-minded ones 'would work obeah on you' or that if you studied too hard you would 'get mad' or 'turn fool fool'. Needless to say, there were the optimists who willed the best for you and continually assured you of their prayers for your progress. Occasionally they put an envelope into your hand with 'something' to help with the expenses at college. They also kept in touch with your progress from time to time. Invariably the most important thing for your senior well-wishers was that you hold your head high, remember the value of good manners and not get distracted by things that are not in your best interest.

In the final analysis, nothing is more helpful to an aspiring young achiever or leader, than the goodwill and support of the community of origin. You ignore or discount this to your own peril. It is extremely difficult, if not impossible, for anyone to become a competent, committed and dependable leader without the affirmation, goodwill, encouragement and constant support of one's village or neighborhood of origin. Those who never received the approval, correction, and encouragement of those who watched them grow up rarely become leaders who can be depended upon to be reliable and persevering. This is particularly so in the context of the socio-religious community.

The leader mirrors the community which is led by him/her. He/she is the bearer of its traditions, its aspirations, even its shortcomings and frustrations. Those who do not meet these criteria, remain on the margin, regardless of the length of their tenure, their skills or the length of their experience. Those who do not represent what the community is and wants to be, may be effective managers but not leaders in the true sense of that word.

By the same token, if one goes from one's community of origin to serve elsewhere without the endorsement of this community of origin, one can hardly hope to become accepted, affirmed or effective whenever one is assigned to lead. Those who cannot go back home or are not known where they are coming from, are hardly likely to get acceptance where they are assigned or appointed to lead, and this is no less true of religious leadership than it is of leadership in non-religious spheres. In the final analysis, it is the people of your community of origin who make you what you are and whose perspective of you determines whether you become a leader or not and how effectively you lead where you happen to get called or appointed to lead. Those who have the responsibility for identifying, endorsing and forming religious leaders would do well to bear this in mind as they select prospective ministers, train them and approve them for ordination, and transfer them from one place to another in the course of their careers.

Leaders in any sphere of reference or social context are persons who enjoy the respect, goodwill, moral support and trust of the families to which they belong, the communities in which they were cradled, nurtured socially, morally, spiritually and attitudinally. Those who do not enjoy the trust of those who make up their communities of origin and formation, almost invariably fail to make the grade in the estimation of those who elect, appoint or endorse them from time to time. In my case, every 'elder' in my community of origin insisted that, like others who have emerged from that particular local community, "I am his or her boy" who has not disappointed. I am the achievement of all those who thought well of me and wished me well as I left them for study and training at the end of each term as a student on vacation or a home boy on a brief visit with parents or local community event. For them what I am, in their, view, is not personal achievement but the personification of some of the ideals and aspirations of peoples and communities who have had access to the bare minimum in terms of economic opportunity and social empowerment. Needless to say, they can be devastated when those in whom they have invested so much, never return home too much nor provide inspiration to places of worth and honour.

Unfortunately, in the cases of persons like myself the older you get the more costly it is to pay the occasional visit back to the village and therefore the longer the time between visits. Fortunately however, because of my children's sense of history I am taken on a trip home at least once a year when they are on vacation and feel obliged to go to the scene of resting places of one set of their great grandparents and grandparents. Their willingness to go back to that set of their own roots, is itself evidence of the right of the community of origin of a leader to share the compliments normally given to those responsible for the preparations for leadership of quality.

Learning 'the work'

I have been a student ever since I became aware of myself as a person. I have not yet come across this in any text on psychology of learning but I am convinced that learning takes place even during sleep. As a child I was told that if one had difficulty with a subject one should put the text book under one's pillow so that what is in the book would become part of one's store of knowledge during sleep.

My formal preparation for the practice of pastoral ministry began in 1950 at St. Colme's College, the Presbyterian Theological Seminary in Jamaica. This institution was located at 5 Lockett Avenue in Kingston Gardens in Central Kingston. Students in residence belonged not only to the Presbyterian Church but also to the Moravian Church in Jamaica and the Congregational Church.

There were just above seven men in residence during the years I spent there but we were just part of a larger student body made up of men and women from Calabar, the Baptist College, Caenwood, and the Methodist College at which the Methodist students from the Caribbean and Central America were trained. During the years 1950-54 there was a member of the Society of Friends in the student body. He lived at Caenwood. He was the only Quaker to be trained in Jamaica. Occasionally the students at Caenwood, Calabar and St. Colme's met with Anglican students who were residents at premises at Cross Roads, at what was known as St. Peter's Theological College. All the theological or ministerial students played in the same cricket or football teams which played against students of other tertiary institutions such as the Mico Teachers College and the Jamaica

School of Agriculture. Occasionally, we played against teams made up of members of the Jamaica Constabulary and other groups made up of young men who were residents in the corporate area.

Studying at that level was quite a challenge for me and it didn't take me long to get myself established as a 'grub' to watch. At the end of the first year I got awards in New Testament Greek and Early Church History. Of course, as I mentioned elsewhere, my academic work attracted the attention of both senior students of the college and my denominational tutor and his compatriots serving the Presbyterian Church as missionaries. My fellow students not only used every opportunity to tell others of my being a 'country bumpkin', they did everything to dissuade me from working hard and getting good grades. Among the things, they did was to make it appear that it was against the rules to keep the lights on in the room after midnight. Another way was to try to persuade me of the dangers of studying at anytime on Sunday, especially if the subject being studied was Greek Grammar or Greek Text. A Scottish person in the field tried to persuade me that too much scholarship was not very helpful for pastoral work in the country, and of course, at that time none of them thought that the day would come when anyone from anywhere in the Caribbean would become either pastors of city churches or members of the faculty of the theological colleges.

As Caribbean students of the era we were inspired by the acting appointment to faculty of a Methodist Minister from Jamaica named Caleb Cousins who taught New Testament Greek and a Baptist Minister named A.E. Brown who taught Church History. And interestingly enough, four students of the period became faculty of the United Theological College of the West Indies (UTCWI) which was established during the 1960's. These were Horace Russell who taught Church History and later became President of the UTCWI, Gladstone Donalds, who became Presbyterian Warden and lecturer in Systematic Theology, Clement Gayle who taught Church History and Homiletics and myself, who was taken on as the first holder of a lectureship endowed by the Lutheran Church in America, to teach a new course entitled Contemporary Trends in Theology, and later, to be appointed President of the College.

When I graduated from St. Colmes Theological College I was more suited for work in a Scottish city than I was to give pastoral care and preach in the deeply rural Jamaican village to which I was sent to begin my first assignment. None of the members of the faculty of the college knew anything about the history, sociology or economics of the villages of Jamaica or anywhere else in the Caribbean. Students for the ministry in these places were expected to learn about contexts during summer and Easter holidays that were spent with the 'native' Ministers who were all in rural parishes. Interestingly enough, there was little or no de-briefing at our college at the end of the breaks. It was as if what we learned or experienced away from the precincts of the college did not matter to those who were preparing us for ordination to the ministry in our respective denominations. Fortunately, most of us had some competent older pastors as our mentors during the brief internships.

I was fortunate to have met as a young Minister in the first five years of ministry, an American Presbyterian Minister named Ray Schember. He was instrumental in my obtaining a bursary at Lancaster Theological Seminary in Pennsylvania and a Fulbright Travel Grant to take care of the costs of travelling. The administration of my church granted me leave to take up the

Scholarship but provided me with no financial support whatever, even though I reported to them on a regular basis. I was able to pay my way during the year out of small honoraria I got from sermons and speeches made in churches during the academic year.

It was at Lancaster Seminary that I was introduced to the study of the dynamics of both rural and urban church leadership and Contemporary Theology. It was while I was there that I acquired a perspective on Jamaica and the challenge of development in a post-colonial situation. It was there for the first time in my life that I was assigned work that required my reading the history of my own country and doing reflection on the social and political challenges inherent in situations like that in Jamaica and the rest of the Caribbean. Jamaica assumed widespread status during my second year of study in the United States of America.

One of the persons who mentored me at Lancaster, Pennsylvania, was Professor Alfred Bartholomew who taught Rural and Urban Sociology and Missiology and was my personal confidant in what was then a racially segregated American city. Pleased with my academic work and adjustment to the American context he recommended me for a research assistantship at the newly established Interdenominational Theological Centre in Atlanta, Georgia.

I paid my airfare to Atlanta out of the salary I earned during the summer as supply pastor at Trinity Presbyterian Church, York, Pennsylvania where my hosts were the Rev. George McCredie and his wife Lois. They were friends of the Rev. Raymond Schember and his wife Alice.

At the Interdenominational Theological Centre I was fortunate to come under the influence of three persons who made much difference in my life. The first was Professor Ralph Williamson who was known to my Jamaican older colleague Clement Thomas who became the first General Secretary of the United Church in Jamaica and the Cayman Islands, Professor and President Harry Richardson who also had met him (Clem Thomas) at Drew University, and Professor Kinchloe, the last of whom got me fascinated with the study of Sociology of Religion, a sub-discipline which transformed by consciousness and perspective on religion in general and Christian Theology in particular.

Professor Williamson was a plodder academically who was delighted to have a student who showed some interest in his research on the Black Church in America. He taught me Research Methods and was my thesis advisor in the area of Church and Society. He helped me to understand the problems related to adjustment of the Black Caribbean person to the Black American Community.

Professor Richardson who was an authority on the Black Church in America gave me invaluable help in my study of myself as a Black leader committed to the empowerment of Black people in a white dominated world. The paper I did for him on my assessment of my emotional and intellectual readiness for pastoral leadership revolutionized my approach to self-development and self-ministry.

Professor Kinchloe who was a product of the University of Chicago's work in Anthropology and Sociology did much to open my eyes to the need to ground theological concepts in social, historical and political reality. My students in courses at the University of the West Indies, and elsewhere, will remember my eagerness to introduce and explain the principle of socio-cultural compatibility each time I dealt with this aspect of the study of Religion and Society. I remember the hours I spent in classes taught by Samuel Kinchloe at the Interdenominational Centre, Atlanta Georgia, 1961-62.

It was at Princeton Theological Seminary, New Jersey, during 1967-68 academic year that I had the privilege of interacting with some of the foremost exponents of what many have come to refer to as Liberation Theology, the Contextualization of Theology and Political Theologies. Names like Richard Shaull, Samuel Blizzard, Seward Hiltner, Charles West, James McCord and James Emerson come to mind, whenever I use certain words related to the making of people and the breaking up of structures of domination and mis-development.

Among the memories of the Princeton experience that I cherish are the following:

a) The sense of solidarity expressed by students from the British Commonwealth of nations some of whom normally avoid all contact with each other in their own country.

b) The variety of responses to the assassination of Civil Rights leader, Martin Luther King.

c) The response I got from a number of leaders of a large all white congregation in Philadelphia on Ascension Sunday, 1968.

I am convinced that my current outlook on globalization, ecumenism and inter-faith

dialogue is derived in no small measure from the experience I gained during my stay on the campus of Princeton Theological Seminary during the 1967-68 academic year. It is a fervent hope that the culture of that context will not only be preserved but also emulated by institutions of that kind all over the world. There is nothing better for a world in which conflict seems to proliferate at a time when human beings interface with each other with such ease and frequency. I consider myself very privileged as far as opportunity for training and continuing education goes. Of course, as I said at the beginning, my education is continuous. Every assignment in any part of the world, every Sabbatical, every symposium abroad or at home, especially when these involve the presentation and discussion of papers and reports, provides opportunity for gaining new insight on some aspect of reality or concepts related to my own professional interests. I am equally grateful to the British Council of Churches which provided me with the similar opportunities during the Michaelmas term of 1987 when along with other theological educators from various regions of the world, I had access to the libraries of British Theological Colleges visited at the invitation of the Council of Churches. The notes I made in libraries and at discussions, have been sources of intellectual enrichment and growth.

Learning the work continues for me. In recent years when I had more time, I had turned my attention to a number of areas of interests that got less attention from me than was necessary, in the height of my career. One of these is human forgiveness as a source of personal liberation, growth and healing and a resource of inter-personal, intergroup and international reconciliation, the plight of men and boys in an era of the ascendency of women and various aspects of the study of African Traditional Religion and African Retentions in the Caribbean and other areas of the Western Hemisphere in which Black Africans have been enslaved and suppressed. Insights from study and reflection in the areas mentioned have contributed immensely to my development as a person and my effectiveness as a teacher and a leader. The books and scholarly papers produced by scholars at the University of the West Indies and Black Scholars of North America and Great Britain, have been of tremendous value to me in my search for answers and the formulation of new questions or issues related to the transformation of the structures of power in our world.

Fighting battles like Elijah

In the first book of Kings there is a story about the prophet sinking into despair because he came to the conclusion that he was alone in the fight against Baalism. There may have been others, who, like himself, saw the evil in what was happening but were too concerned with personal security not sufficiently aware of faithfulness of dependability of Yahweh. Of course, in the depth of his despair it was revealed to them that there were thousands all over the nation of like mind who had not 'bowed the knee to Baal'.

There have always been times in my life since the time when I began to prepare formally for work in the church, when I have been obsessed with the feeling that I am alone in the fight against some form of injustice or another. Perhaps the most challenging of all these is the prevalence of the influence of Euro-theology, the most pernicious aspect of which is the notion that there are levels of responsibility in the work of the Church with which "natives" cannot be entrusted in the immediate time, of course, for those who hold that view, the appointed time is always in the distant future which is another way of describing what is meant by the word NEVER.

In my time it was alright for the majority of my colleagues to talk about these things, out of the hearing of the seniors, but dangerous to mention them in open discussion. They were always afraid of being marked for victimization or even expulsion. We very often hear the story of the Minister who had to leave the Presbyterian ministry in Jamaica because of his preaching a sermon entitled 'Men with Backbone'. In that instance the 'rebel' native was not even given the opportunity to appeal, and there is no record of any protest by his fellow colonial subjects, the 'native', pastors and synod elders.

When the warden/tutor of the Presbyterian Theological College withheld my diploma because the same examination for the London University diploma which I was sitting, coincided with those of the college, no one raised the issue anywhere so I ended up not getting a diploma even though I was a student of more than 'average ability' and had earned the diploma in Theology from the University. All those who were in a position to raise the issue, either did not care enough, or did not want to 'rock the boat' and this, is out of the fear of losing the sponsorship of 'mother church'.

Something similar took place when in my position of Chairman of the Ministerial Training Committee of the United Church in Jamaica and Grand Cayman, I insisted the retiring Scottish Warden of the United Church students at the United Theological College of the West Indies should not be succeeded by an overseas person, my senior colleagues responded very tamely that there was no national on the horizon who was suitably qualified to take in the responsibility of warden and lecturer in Systematic Theology. Because of my insistence, the church agreed to the leave the position vacant until a national had earned a master's degree in Systematic Theology at what they referred to as a reputable Theological institution. Of course, just as some thought the 'Fathers' of the Church of Scotland responded to that move by weening the national church. This took the form of the removal of any subsidy for the theological education or any other areas of the church's ministry that had enjoyed the sponsorship of 'mother church' for over a hundred years. An interesting feature of that episode is that it was the Church of Scotland that took the initiative towards reconciliation between the two churches. One of the conditions of the new arrangement was that in future there be an exchange of personnel rather than the traditional 'sending' and 'receiving' of resources and personnel with the sending and receiving always at the same ends. One of the church's worst flaws is the traditional tendency of leaders at various levels to either 'cover up' or 'play down' flaws or blatant sins which in secular terms are nothing short of crimes. This approach is due largely to the penchant for perfectionism among Christians, something that is really evidence of theological misguidedness. Many Christians are completely unaware of the essence of the teachings of Jesus as against those of fundamentalist Jews.

One aspect of fundamentalism is perfectionism. This implies, among other human things, the notions that the religious faithful is immune to sin and error of any kind. Followers of the Christian faith tend to forget that Jesus accepted persons (including his twelve disciples) with all of their imperfections, and expect, those who are committed to his teachings to do so likewise. It is certainly because of this on the part of Jesus, that he could have had as his close associates angry daggermen, racial exclusionists, patriarchists and former extortioners.

Because of this perfectionist and traditionalist tendency among Christians, most Christian leaders are resistant to attempts to follow the approach of Jesus as it applies to the matter of objective and unconditional justice. This is why blatant injustice against women, non-Europeans and younger persons, has gone on in churches for so long. Even in churches in which women are eligible for ordination and election to decision making bodies, there is still a tendency for women to be overlooked for certain benefits that go along with employment packages. In not a few cases female employees of the Church are denied housing allowances that are normally paid to men, when they share residence with spouses or other relatives. I incurred the anger of many of my seniors once when I insisted that a deaconess who was living at the residence of a relative be paid the housing allowance that would normally be paid to her male counterpart, since in the current arrangement her relative was being made to carry part of the responsibility of the denomination in addition to her personal obligations to the congregation to which she belonged. My older colleagues felt that I was taking the matter of gender injustice too far. The person in question was discriminated against in respect of housing allowance until her retirement, over twenty years beyond the time I drew attention to the injustice on patriarchal grounds.

One who is sensitive in matters of ethics and morality can become impatient with the behavior and decisions of those who represent the 'powers that be' and tempted to become hopeless as far as the practice of justice goes. However, one must be patient while being activist and hopeful for change. The stories of Elijah, Esther, Jesus, Gandhi, Martin Luther King, Nelson Mandela and other martyrs of causes, help to strengthen our hope and prevent us from becoming irrational and destructively angry. In my own case this approach has helped me to discover that there are always many 'secret disciples' out there who share my convictions but who elect to remain silent for a host of reasons. Many persons of goodwill whose voices are never heard, keep pounding away at the evil, in the hope of opening up the situation to change for the better. They are aware also that situations that are currently closed, restrictive and oppressive, affect not only obvious victims but also the perpetrators who are themselves trapped in structures of injustice and therefore remain spiritually and morally stunted. Elijahs of any day need to revisit Jesus' parable of The Seed growing secretly, recorded in the fourth chapter of the Gospel according to Mark (vs. 26-29).

What I have grown to understand through reflection and reading, is that God's will in respect of justice, will not only be done inevitably but also become manifestly so. What is most interesting is how easily those, who now support or even merely tolerate injustice, identify with the most desirable outcome of the struggle for change only when it is no longer risky to do so.

In my own struggle against injustice within the context of the Christian Church in which I was cradled, nurtured and ordained, there is a lady named Marjorie Saunders who has always been outspoken on issues of justice involving issues of race, class and gender. As a leader in the church, she had never been afraid to articulate her feelings and her plan to change prevailing situations so that they may conform to principles articulated by Jesus in the Sermon on the Mount.

In Madge Saunders' case, much of what she agitated for, during her long career, has been achieved in her lifetime. She came to be referred to as 'Mother' of the contemporary United Church in Jamaica and the Cayman Islands.

Older members of the United Church will remember the days when the Rev. Madge Saunders as Director of the Women's Movement and organizer of youth work in the former Presbyterian Church in Jamaica, did not have the right to speak on the floor of either Synod or Presbytery. Women who are now Ministers of the church and elders in congregations, need to be aware of this and that much of the gender equality that is now a feature of the life of our church must be credited to the advocacy of one who was once a 'voice crying in the wilderness'.

As a crusader for justice in church and society I remain indebted to Madge Saunders for the support she gave to me when many of my male contemporaries were too timid to take on the prophets of 'Baal'. An interesting aspect of the partnership between myself and Madge Saunders is that both of us were privileged to come under the tutelage of a less combative but effective crusader named John Samuel Wint. She came under the influence of the burly Presbyterian Minister at Port Maria, St. Mary and I at Blauwearie, Westmoreland, a part of the Brownsville Charge where "Big John" was the pastor, decades after he left Port Maria.

An area of the church's witness in which my commitment had put me at cross purposes with fellow Christians, is the witness in elective politics. Because of the influence of my father who was at different times a preaching deacon in the local Baptist church and a preaching elder in the local Presbyterian church, and at the same time, actively engaged in the partisan politics of the day, I saw no inconsistencies whatever, in being totally immersed in the politics of the development and change while being a faithful follower of the teachings of Christ. Of course, not many of my ministerial colleagues, throughout most of my career, felt free to go along with me. Happily, however, before the beginning of the second millennium, not only Ministers of mainline churches but mainly in the Pentecostal and other Evangelical Churches were not only supportive of my position on politics but openly engaged in politics often as candidates for election and card-carrying members of political parties. It is my view that there were always those who were secretly supportive of my position in respect of the struggles of governance in this world but like the undeclared supporters of Elijah and later Jesus, elected to play it safe until the situation for them looked less perilous.

What is true of my position on the issues of the public sphere has been the same in respect of issues like the contextualization of the language of Christian Theology. When a colleague in the Diaspora heard that I was teaching a course entitled Contemporary Theologies at the UTCWI expressed skepticism about the appropriateness of making reference to varieties of Theology or even the concept of other theologies in reputable centers of learning especially in North America, the fears of that particular colleague were allayed when he was told by an overseas colleague that there were courses with such designations in the curricula of theological institutions in the western world. Needless to say, it took someone from the North to convince him that what I was introducing in our context was not only valid but also valid and timely.

The situation within the church in respect of my credibility as a representative of established Christianity in Jamaica became even more precarious when papers I wrote on aspects of the contemporary situation in the political development of the region, were published in newspapers and periodicals.

Among other things, I was asking Christians to take seriously what was being said by Rastafarians and non-rastafarians exponents of 'Black Power', a slogan which conveyed the depth of the impatience of victims of Euro-colonization and racism, especially in North America and the Caribbean.

Reference has been made elsewhere to a scenario in which a fellow black Jamaican Church leader who rebuked me publicly for raising the 'Black Power' issue in the public sphere, was himself openly rebuked by a white colleague of his own denomination for failing to support me in a matter which he, an Englishman, thought worthy of urgent attention on the part of those who spoke for the

Christian church at that juncture in the history of the country and the church.

I earned the ire of perhaps more middle of the road and typically cautious middle class Christians in Jamaica when after the General Elections in 1992 which was won by the People's National Party, I accepted the invitation of Prime Minister Michael Manley to be his advisor on Religious affairs. Even those who would have voted for the governing party question the appropriateness of a religious leader being openly associated with the shaping of government policy on anything. Many of the critics of Michael Manley's socialist outlook went as far as to describe me as "communist". In my own denomination many withdrew their support for the church because senior colleagues did not publicly condemn me for not following the tradition of staying clear of anything that smacked of partisan politics.

Because of my involvement not only with the United Church in Jamaica and the Cayman Island but also with the Jamaica Council of Churches and the Caribbean Conference of Churches and none of these organizations had publicly repudiated the politics of Michael Manley, the eyes of large numbers of Christians who are usually theologically conservative, became very suspicious of all ecumenical organizations and agencies. One of the consequences of this was that many members of mainline denominations withdrew their membership from Churches in which they were cradled and nurtured and became associated with churches that followed a theology that supported the view that elective politics is forbidden territory for committed Christians.

At the time of writing nearly four decades after the beginning of the Michael Manley era of Jamaican politics, very few representatives of the churches of whatever brand of theology, raise eyebrows at any mention of subjects like Caribbean Theology, Liberation Theology, Feminist or Womanist Theology or the indigenization of language about God.

Many erstwhile conservative Christians now register for courses at the University of the West Indies dealing with subjects like

African Traditional Religions, African Religious Retentions in the Caribbean. All of this is because, increasingly Christians and others who have been politically conservative, have become less ashamed of referring to matters of faith and social issues in their own tongue and in relation to their own ethnic origins and class interests.

By the same token, and increasingly, even in traditional euro-based churches, adherents and leaders appear in garbs that reflect the non-European ancestry and approve the use of musical instruments and liturgical forms which are in keeping with the culture and historical experience of their victimized ancestors.

The situation in Jamaica and indeed, throughout the Caribbean, in respect of what is referred to as socio-theology, is today, a far cry from what was in the 1970s and '80s when those who spoke of God and things related to the Christian faith in words other than those approved by planters and missionaries in the period between the advent of Christopher Columbus in the 15th century and the inception of the process of the de-europeanisation of the church especially in the anglo-phone Caribbean in the early 1960s, were viewed with suspicion .

As far as the aspect of the process of the de-colonisation is concerned, undeclared prophets of Yahweh and secret disciples of Jesus on the issues of justice and liberation now have no need to remain in hiding or denial. Persons like myself now feel legitimized, with all our unworthiness and shortcomings, even where we have been called to lead the change in situations where it was very costly to be in front. Students of the history of the Caribbean church know well that Christians are no less vengeful and cowardly than their brothers and sisters in other religions and other areas of social relationships.

Christlike openness is so seldom taken into account by those who feel obliged to silence or betray those who dare to deviate from established orthodoxy; the latter are sometimes not only ostracized or sidelined, some have been stoned or burned at the stake.

Fortunately, many who have been dealt with most severely in their lifetime have been canonized or beatified long after their demise. In my case, I have had the good fortune of hearing in my lifetime that I have been just a little "ahead of my time".

My reading of the writings of the apostles on subjects like faithfulness of invisible hosts of martyrs who have preceded them into glory, and more recently my readings of African Traditional Religions, have helped me to arrive at a place in my spiritual development which I can be convinced of having the support of all the faithful with me at all times. Needless to say, that applies to all who like Elijah of old have had reason to feel that they only are left to face the enemy who seems invincible.

Moral support for me has come from countless numbers of persons known and unknown to me ever since I began to take positions on which I have failed to get or retain the support of those on whom I should have been able to depend.

Most of my support of unpopular issues has come from ordinary lay persons in the church and men on the street who have sometimes naively identified with me because they have perceived themselves as being victims of the situations I have committed myself to changing. My Irish colleagues who have worked in Jamaica have also been very supportive. One person to whom I owe a great debt of gratitude is a former President of the Interdenominational Theological Centre, Atlanta Georgia, where I was a graduate student and research assistant in the 1961-62 academic year. It was President Harry Richardson who during a conversation with him over a paper I had written for him in a course he taught, told me I should commit my thoughts to writing because in his view I had literary gifts. He and a Jamaican journalist and former editor of a weekly publication in Jamaica, Len Nembhard, who became a parishioner at one of the churches I served, urged me to put my thoughts on paper and seek publication for what I wrote. I have been embolden by the response to work that I have written and had published in various publications between the late sixties and the present time. Ironically the same ideas that were earning my enemies in some quarters were winning me admirers and supporters in others.

In the final analysis, it was from members of classes I taught at the UTCWI that I got most encouragement in my determination to change the self-perception of the victims of the injustices of church and society, and the world views of those who were associated with the perpetrators of these evils over half a century after I ventured on any crusade of change. I am able to say in print and verbally that much of the mission on which persons like myself have embarked especially in relation to the witness of the Christian church, has been accomplished. What makes me doubly thankful is that in response to the challenge of persons like President Harry Richardson of the Interdenominational Theological Centre, Richard Shaull of Princeton Theological Seminary and former parishioners like 'Father' Clarence Skeete of Jones Town and Wilford Daley of Franklyn Town, Kingston, and scores of enlightened ordinary and virtually unlettered poor Jamaican men and women, I have lived to see some of my dreams for a more humanized world fulfilled. Even more importantly I have lived to see the efforts of persons like myself supported by many who have opposed them vehemently even twenty years ago. For this I consider myself more fortunate than many of my role models like Mahatma Gandhi, Marcus Garvey, Martin Luther King, Norman Manley, C.L.R. James and John Samuel Wint, to name only a few, by whose efforts to change the world, I have been greatly inspired.

I find very few activities as challenging as those related to the mentoring of students in tertiary institutions especially in the study of religion and the behavior of religious persons and the concerns of persons and groups about questions of 'ultimate concern'. Among other things, it challenges one to remain alert and abreast of what is taking place in academia and wherever else persons and groups wrestle with existential, relational and theological questions

Encountering Racism in Church

Before my twenty-first birthday I had interfaced with less than ten 'white' persons and most of those persons were Scottish missionaries and their spouses. I saw and heard those persons mostly on special occasions in the Presbyterian congregations when they were invited as special visitors. Of course, in those days such persons were invited because it was known that the intention of their appearance was to pull crowds who delighted in seeing and hearing foreigners.

In those early days of my life and association with the church, missionaries seldom shook hands with anyone in the local church apart from the host minister, his wife and one or two highly favoured local lay persons, and in many instances, the visiting lady wore gloves. I later learned that many of these overseas persons did not accept the hospitality of local folk. They brought everything with them from their own home. Some of this is understandable now, but it was worrying and even annoying in the days when it was prevalent.

When I became a ministerial student I learned before long that if a national wishes to survive as a candidate for ordination he should be careful about disagreeing with the missionary on campus or anywhere else, since there would be no hope of getting the support of nationals in the hierarchy of the church, in case one had to defend ones' self against a charge brought against one by a senior person, white or black. Very few nationals dared to challenge the word of a missionary openly in those days.

In the synod of the Presbyterian Church those who participated in the discussions were designated 'missionaries', 'ministers', and elders.

In fact, missionaries of the Church of Scotland were not inducted by the officers of the Presbyteries because the local or 'receiving' church had no jurisdiction over the person sent by the overseas churches. The first overseas minister to be inducted by our church was a Canadian and this took place only in 1963. Missionaries were 'introduced' to congregations to which they were sent directly and they were accountable only to those who sent them. They were maintained directly by those who sent them and answerable only to them.

There was really no difference between the overseas missionary and the colonial civil servant. I began to discern traces of ethno-ecclesiastical discrimination and arrogance and the practice of the containment of 'native' clergy when the denominational warden of the United Theological College expressed hesitancy about permitting students under his jurisdiction to prepare for external examinations in divinity set in those days by the University of London. My warden was careful in explaining to us that we were being prepared for leadership of the congregations in rural villages and neither for the city congregations nor teaching in the Theological College. In fact, in those days congregations of my denomination in the capital city and large towns would accept ministers only from Great Britain. Those from North America were deemed not to have the right accent or scholastic depth.

It was only after much negotiation that one of my seniors was allowed to prepare for the overseas examination and in my case, I had great difficulty obtaining the requisite forms of application from overseas authorities. When I got an opportunity to do postgraduate studies overseas, officials of the Synod ordered me home to fill one of the vacancies created by retirements and deaths. On my return home I was told that it was the ministerial tutor who had persuaded them to have me curtail my study leave because in his view, there was no need in the church for ministers with graduate or post graduate degrees, since such qualification would be for teaching purposes and there were no vacancies in the college at that time.

Ironically, just about a year after my return, in a response to an expression of appreciation, my former tutor who was leaving for an appointment in North America, remarked that if he had nothing else to show for his work in Jamaica he had Ashley Smith. He was obviously pleased that his erstwhile troublesome student had turned out to be someone of whom, as a teacher, he had need to be proud and hopeful.

When the widow of my former tutor returned to Jamaica nearly forty years later as a special guest at the service marking the centenary of the church at which the husband served as pastor while being the theological tutor nearly fifty years before, she greeted me warmly as his past student, who, in addition to being a past minister at the same congregation, had served for many years at the theological seminary as a lecturer, Vice President and President, consecutively. At the time of her visit there was not one of the former Presbyterian congregations that was pastored by the representative of a British or North American mission board.

An interesting feature of the transition in the Church from missionary leadership to national leadership was the obvious absence of white persons in the lay leadership of congregations. The pattern in all mainline denominations with long traditions of overseas leadership is that whenever the congregation calls or is assigned a resident pastor who is black, white or near-white members either drop out of membership or become only minimally involved. In many cases these persons become members of independent congregations that remain independent in order to ensure that for as long as possible, they 'enjoy' the privilege of having pastors that are neither 'native' nor 'Black'. Of course, throughout the history of the church in the Caribbean region, it has been very rare for a local white person to offer for full-time ministry and either get trained locally or return to work in his or her own country after being trained abroad. In most cases white or near-white recruits for Christian Ministry either stay abroad after being trained and ordained or return as 'missionary' serving under the aegis of an overseas mission board.

Discerning persons in all mainline denominations tell stories of encounters with racism in their churches at various points in their history. What is most interesting about this issue is that in many cases those who usually object to 'native' or 'Black' pastors are themselves 'flag' black. In most denominations the strongest objection is to the spouse of the pastor who does not have the 'right colour'. This writer was told by a teenage youngster many years ago that the members of the rural congregation (who were nearly all black) did not like black ministers but did not mind me because I was 'tall'. Women who were members of that congregation said that their first really 'black' minister would have been more acceptable if his wife had 'better hair' and did not work for a salary outside of the manse or the ministers' residence.

The situation in other denominations was no different from what it was in the Presbyterian church. A Jamaican Roman Catholic priest of blessed memory, told how many members of his first parish stayed away from mass for many weeks after his appointment there, because they were not ready to receive the 'host' from a 'black hand'. Many of these persons transferred to congregations that had white priests.

A very interesting case of racism in the Jamaican church is that of a missionary pastor who adopted a black Jamaican child. When the first Jamaican national of the church with which he worked was appointed presiding minister, he visited a fellow missionary pastor to advise him that he was leaving for another country because he was not yet ready to be led by a black person. One of the interesting things about that story is that the person under whose leadership he was not ready to serve was one who could 'pass for white' in Jamaica and he was making his announcement in the presence of a third person to whom Professor Rex Nettleford would refer as 'flag' black.

There are reports of overseas persons refusing to send their children to local church camps because they did not want their children to be exposed to 'native' children for extended periods away from the presence of persons who look like their parents and shared their cultural characteristics and values.

My own encounters with racism in the Church has been at theological institutions overseas. At the first Seminary I attended, I was the only 'Black student' and the second black person to be admitted there in over a hundred years. The first one was Ghanian.

Many of the students were from Southern States. One admitted to me that he and some of his compatriots were avoiding sitting at the dining table with me, and sometimes returned to their rooms if on entering the dining room they observed that the only table with vacant places was the one at which I was sitting. Such students would either negotiate with another student for an exchange of place or leave the room. When one of the offending students got to know me better, in addition to commending me for not being a 'run of the mill black man', he admitted that he was told as a child to be kind to black people but never to sit at a table with a black person. When that student brought his fiancé to the common room once, he introduced her to the other two students standing with me and ignored me completely. Just about a year after that he made up for it. Members of his year group invited me to spend the weekend on the campus. He volunteered to come to meet me at the airport. He not only brought his wife but insisted that I sit with them in the front seat although no one occupied the back seat. While we had a meal in the restaurant he told me he had volunteered to come and fetch me at the airport because he wanted to use the opportunity to demonstrate to me that he had overcome his aversion to black persons.

At another theological seminary there was a student on the floor of the hall on which I lived. Who would never greet me or any other foreign non-white student first. When I greeted him often when we met in the hallway, he merely 'grunted' a response but made sure not to speak to me or any of the Koreans who lived on the same floor. On one occasion when we met in the room of another student he refused to take a cookie from the plate offered by a Korean student but when the same plate was extended by a white student, he accepted. Needless to say, that person was just months away from the date of his ordination to the Christian Ministry.

I was told by a member of the student body of the first seminary I referred to, of an incident in which members of a church hosting the seminary choir refused to have the only black student as overnight guest. It was not until during the welcome to the Seminary choir, it was mentioned that the Black student was a visitor from Africa, that the members of the church were willing to have him as their guest. Members of the host choir were overheard expressing the hope that in the future they would not have to sit in the seat occupied by the 'black' member of the Seminary choir.

Blacks who travel to countries of the north or Far East might save themselves a lot of pain by accepting the theory that the membership in or adherence to any religion does not guarantee automatic acceptance by those who are deemed to be outsiders and therefore not deserving of full acceptance by those who claim the right to exclude and/or include whom they will, when and where they choose to do so. The history of Christendom is replete with illustrations of the fact that religious convictions are not synonymous with moral commitment and moral values are never universal. This is why leaders of theological thought like Martin Luther King, assert that the church usually changes only after change in respect of certain social and moral norms take place in other areas of social and political life. This means that, by and large, there is always disparity between the ideals of the Christian faith and the practice of those who claim to be Christian. And, nowhere is this more obvious than in matters related to race, class and the exercise of political authority. Genuine discipleship is always costly and the pre-crucifixion Peter of the New Testament record, is always a feature of the personality of all who have pledged to follow the way of Christ. There are layers of our being that we keep under wraps, not because we ae insincere or wicked, but just because he best of us remains 'adamic' even after sincere commitment to Christ.

The experience of post-Pentecost Peter does not come automatically to all who at 'confirmation' or reception into membership or believers' baptism pledge to be loyal to Christ.

The fears in which racial prejudices are rooted, are overcome only by the power of the Holy Spirit and not without pain and sometimes, shame.

Thankfully, many have had the experience of being freed or liberated from their prejudices, and therefore, there is ground for hoping that there will be less of this evil in the future.

Racism is perhaps the most formidable obstacle to the propagation of the Gospel in any part of the world. Of course, it is well known by students of missiology and the Bible, that as in the case of Jonah the prophet, the effectiveness of efforts at evangelization do not depend entirely on the racial attitude or moral maturity of those who happen to be the 'bearers of good news'. God's will is done not only because of but also (and perhaps more likely) in spite of the human agent involved.

The history of Christian missionary activities is replete with stories that illustrate the belief that what God wills for God's world, can be accomplished, despite the disobedience or ignorance of those who happen to be instruments in God's hand. However, this does not make something like racism less sinful and its perpetrators less accountable to God and the victims of their arrogance and disobedience.

In fairness to Euro-Christians, and in the interest of truth and justice, it must be emphasized that racism is by no means peculiar to Europeans or Euro-Americans and it is not less sinful when practiced by Asians, Latin-Americans, by Africans against representatives of other ethnic groups, other classes or other tribes.

In my own denomination, nationals have been very cowardly in their approach to racism. It is as if they feel that it is improper or unchristian even to discuss the subject in the presence of white colleagues. As far as I can remember, most times when the issue is raised in open discussion by anyone other than myself, it has been by overseas whites, especially citizens of Ireland, Canada and the United States of America. Irish persons and Canadians known to me have been quite open in their criticism of the persistence of subtle racism in the Jamaican church. At least three of them are on record for declining appointments to traditional 'missionary charges' in deference to their black national colleagues.

On one occasion when I wrote about the need for Jamaican Christians to look at racism in the church, I was openly rebuffed by the Black leader of another denomination who not only apologized in the interest of the whites whom he thought would have been offended by what I wrote, but openly denounced me as 'not showing more wisdom than Rastafarians'. He was taken on in the press not only by Rastafarians who were offended by his insinuation, but interestingly, by an English brother in his own denomination, who not only apologized on behalf of that denomination, but commended me for opening up the subject for public discussion, especially among the leaders of the churches.

On another occasion, when I raised the issue in a presentation at a retreat of leaders of my own denomination, all the black nationals sat there seemingly embarrassed by what I did on that occasion. It was an Irish brother, who broke that silence and freed up the situation for a discussion that turned out to be cathartic. He began by saying that he was relieved to hear someone like myself address this matter, which, in his view, urgently needed to be explored. He spoke of the embarrassment he felt when on his first visit with the choir of the church he was serving as pastor, he was told by a dark skinned member of the group how pleased she was that it was someone like himself and not a black national who was to be their new minister. He was not quite certain how to respond to her but wondered why this black woman thought the minister of her congregation should never be the same ethnic type or nationality as herself.

It was after the intervention of this enlightened white colleague that my fellow nationals felt free to express their own feelings on this matter about which many of them were secretly angry and impatient with what obtained in the church.

Despite increasing openness on the issue by a few of us, there were many who were of the view that nationals, who were all Black, were not ready to take over. A representative of the Church of Scotland who visited Jamaica in the late 1970's told the General Secretary of the Denomination and myself that a majority of the older Jamaica ministers with whom he had spoken during his visit, were still of the view that at least one of the city pulpits should be reserved for a representative of the Church of Scotland.

In the case of another prominent city of Kingston congregation, something rather interesting took place. After the congregation voted to have a black national as their first non-missionary pastor, a number of the members petitioned the Council (Presbyterian) with a view to having the decision to call rescinded. Those who signed the petition were mostly dark skinned men who cited the Minister's politics as one of the reasons for their apprehensiveness about that appointment. In those days anyone who dared to be even mildly critical of the prevailing Euro-Christianity, was accused by the more conservative in the church, the media, and the society at large, of being communist or supportive of the Black Power movement. This is one way of saying that it is unbecoming of a Christian to deal with an issue that contributes to spiritual stagnation.

This writer has lived long enough to hear some of the erstwhile opponents of decolonization of the church apologize for not understanding what the advocacy for the de-Europeanisation of the leadership of the church was about. I remember someone, now of 'blessed memory', confessing to me how angry she was with me, at first, but how much she had come to appreciate the need for what was being done and in addition, how much her own spiritual development had been hindered by her accepting without question, a situation in which she was required to accept the notion of her own inferiority as being in keeping with the will of God. That lady not only came to see the need for resistance of the status quo in the church but also to become a member of the congregation of which I was pastor at the time. It was my privilege to be the presiding minister at the funeral of no less than three members of her family of origin.

Persistence of the preference for white leadership in the church in Jamaica and the rest of the Caribbean at the present time, is due not so much to racial bias on the part of mission boards or influence of the erstwhile white and brown ruling class, as to the prevalence of self-contempt on the part of Blacks. Of course, much of this is due not to the centuries of the preaching and practice of the subordination of non-white peoples, but also to the notion that people of colour are held under curse by God as implied in the story in Genesis chapter ten (20-28) in which God is reported to have pronounced a curse on Ham or Canaan who is said to be the ancestor of Black Africans.

That myth has not only been used by European philosophers and theologians in support of their attitude of contempt for people of colour but also internalized by the victims, most of whom attribute all of these to the will of God. Both the perpetrators and the victims fail to see the distinction between God per se and notions of God which come out of cultural, social and political contexts.

I remain grateful for what I have been able to contribute to the reduction of racism in the Church not only to enlightened fellow victims but also to courageous white fellow-Christians and others who sometimes endanger their own lives and career prospects by daring to support what is just truly civilized and Christ-like.

For my own maturation in dealing with racism especially within the community of the Christian Church, I owe a great deal to my many hosts, fellow students and ministerial colleagues (mostly white) in the Unites States, but especially to the people of Ireland. My wife and I were privileged to be invited by the Presbyterian Church in Ireland in the summer of 1973 to serve as pastor at large as part of the Mission in Reverse Project between that church and my own. It was while in Ireland that I learned that racism was not just about the relationship between blacks and whites or Asians and Blacks but also between whites and whites even in the same country. Some persons, the Irish for instance, speak with their own relationship with the Scottish and English as a 'black' problem without the colour. Some of the stories told by Irish Catholics of Anglo-protestants of Great Britain, sound much like the stories told by Blacks in the American states like Alabama and Mississippi about the indignities suffered by them over many decades at the hands of conservative white Christians.

Much of the anger I lived with, especially after my experience on a Seminary Campus after the assassination of Martin Luther King Jnr., was identified and dealt with effectively by me as I heard the story of the Irish people of their own experience of discrimination, marginalization and suppression, by their fellow whites of the same nationality. Eventually my anger subsided, my vision of the world broadened and my capacity for global ministry was greatly enhanced.

Thanks, especially to my Irish colleagues who had worked in Jamaica where they also learned to live with their fellow British whom they found more difficult to live with before their sojourn in Jamaica.

After many years of encountering racism and hearing about its practice and demoralizing effects on peoples and entire societies, I am convinced that it is one of the world's major problems along with religious bigotry and greed. I am equally convinced that much has been done not only by the members of the victimized groups but also by enlightened members of groups usually associated with its practice and perpetuation. Much has been written on the evil of racism, especially by American academics and human rights activists and their counterparts in places like South Africa and Latin America. By the same token, it can be said that much has changed in race relations especially since the second half of the twentieth century. To victims and potential victims of this evil, changes for the better have taken place in response to protests and skillful negotiations by victim-leaders like Marcus Garvey, Martin Luther King and Nelson Mandela. Persons like myself, however can testify of the efforts made often at great sacrifice and serious risks to themselves and members of their families, of members of the groups usually identified with perpetuators of the evil. Without the involvement of such persons much less would have been accomplished by way of the reduction of the incidence of racial discrimination and oppression as in my case. I must in all honesty attribute most of my own awareness of the dynamics of racism to white American professors and students and my hosts in both the Northern and Southern regions of the United States between 1961 and 1992 during my sojourn in many different contexts in the sub-continent. It is out of those experiences that I have derived much of my current understanding of the pernicious global evil. Thanks to courageous persons who have been my hosts, teachers and fellow students, in places like Lancaster, Philadelphia and York, Pennsylvania; Cincinnati, Ohio; Houston, Texas; Atlanta, Georgia and at institutions like Lancaster Theological Seminary, Pennsylvania, Princeton Theological Seminary, New Jersey, Interdenominational Theological Centre and Columbia Theological Seminary, Atlanta,

Georgia, and to the workers and lecturers in several theological colleges of Great Britain who hosted me during a tour of those institutions in 1988 sponsored by the British Council of Churches.

Without the affirmation, collaboration and the courageous and principled approach of white persons of the same standing in the context referred to, attempts on the part of victims to reduce the incidence of racial discrimination would be futile and at best much less effective than has been the case in parts of the world. I, for one, would have remained much less hopeful of the possibility of the arrival of the day when in the words of the late Martin Luther King, persons would be judged by the quality of their character rather than the colour of their skin. Persons of colour who have not lived in areas of the world like North America, need to be helped to understand how costly it is for white persons especially in suburbs and rural areas to identify with efforts to eliminate racial discrimination and promote relationships that are just and based on the practice of disinterested love. I consider myself fortunate in being able to say that I have seen significant changes for the better, in race relations in many parts of the world including my own country especially since the mid-1960's of the 20th Century. Needless to say, however, there is still much more work to be done and therefore there is no justification for complacency.

On the issue of the prevalence of racial discrimination by Christians those who have been liberated and enlightened whether as erstwhile perpetuators and beneficiaries or victims, need to use all the spiritual resources at their disposal to help others to understand the paradoxical relationship between religious beliefs and commitment and social and cultural orientations and the importance of personal security. Exponents of the Sociology of Religion make reference to socio-cultural compatibility which in the simplest terms mean the ways in which the various elements of life in social contexts fit into each other despite convictions held by some as to what is right or wrong, just or unjust, godly or ungodly. What is interesting about these victims of discrimination of one sort or another, is the ease with which victims in one situation allow themselves to be perpetrators in other situations. For instance the upper middle class black is as likely to be contemptuous of lower class blacks as whites are likely to be in respect of non-whites of one class or custom. By the same token, East Indian Christians are as hesitant about associating with Afro-Caribbean or African Christians in the Caribbean or in Great Britain, as white Christians are, in respect of all persons of colour or white lower classes or persons who speak with other accents. One remembers well the story told of the lower class white American who spoke of being hateful of two classes of persons, those who discriminate against others, and 'blacks'.

It has long been established that religious affiliation or assent to creedal statements, is no guarantee as to how a follower of a religious tradition is likely to behave in certain circumstances. There is also no difference between Christians and non-Christians on matters of social preferences, personal tastes, leisure time activity, choice of life partners or citizenship changes. For individuals, these areas of personal experience, are always painful, sometimes very costly and might be described as conversion experiences. It must be for this reason that Jesus counselled against being judgmental towards those who are currently in error and about loving the neighbor without condition.

One of the interesting things about the practice of racial discrimination is that most of those who are guilty of it are not necessarily aware that they are, and can see no good reason for changing. This means that there is a lot of hard work still to be done on the part of those who have a vision of a world in which fellow human beings are accepted and loved just as they happen to be at the present time and not have unconditional love withheld from them until they become likeable to those who matter.

Living on the Margin of Community and Church

From my earliest years as a boy in the village, at school or in local church, I have never been at the center of things. My earliest 'playmates' who happen to be alive at the time of writing, will recall their being unable to get me to join them on their trips to places away from the home base, where they could be engaged in activities that would not necessarily be approved by parents. After a time they came to the conclusion that my parents did not want their children to get mixed up with those that weren't going anywhere. Of course, some of them would have got this from their parents, many of whom saw my father as someone who wasn't from the district and therefore 'did not mesh with the regular crowd'.

It was the same at school. Because my father was a nationalist who was liberated from the fatalism that was typical of the villagers all across Jamaica in the period of the 1930's and 40's, he insisted that his children make the best use of the opportunity they had of achieving high levels of formal education. As the eldest of his children therefore, I had to make sure to stay ahead of the class at all levels. This means that I should manage my time so that I could have enough time for productive work on the family farm, appreciable performance in sports and in activities at the church.

By the time I got into mid-teens it was not only my parents who expected me to be other than 'run of the mill'. The teachers did and so also the leaders of the local churches (my mother's, and my father's). According to them, one or two needed to be leaders. By the time I got into the late teens or young adulthood, even those villagers and relatives who would have been offended at my being different from the rest of the boys, came to accept the need for one or two to be examples for the rest.

At theological college I very early found myself on the margin because of the position I manifested as a student against 'missionary' hegemony in respect of faculty and senior positions in the churches. From time to time, utterances by fellow students and older pastors caused me to become apprehensive about being able to count on the support of peers and fellow colonial subjects for my anti-colonial outlook and my insistence on helping to change the status quo. The decision of the Principal of the denominational college to withhold my diploma because the time for some final examinations clashed with those of the external examinations which I elected to take, left me with no doubt about my being carefully watched by the people with the clout, in my church. Of course, what concerned me most was not only that I was being subtly contained by representatives of the colonial church but rather, that I was not able to count on the support of fellow colonial subjects

Because of the nature of my formation as citizen, leader and professional, I have never been fully convinced of being an authentic insider, and therefore, I was delighted to hear from one of my intellectual mentors, Professor Errol Miller of the University of the West Indies, that most of the ideas that have contributed significantly to the development of the peoples throughout human history, have come from persons on the margin. Needless to say, being on the margin can be very painful and certainly very lonely and costly. By the same token, it might be asked: What would our world be like were there not the few who have decided to remain on the margin in the interest of what is just, right, and true?

Out of an intellectual and spiritual background as that described above, it should be quite understandable that my ecclesiastical outlook throughout my career should be characterized by openness and maturity, rather than cautiousness, exclusivity or conservatism. It is out of the theological background in which both student body and faculty were of diverse origins, that I have come with the readiness to listen to and have fellowship with my brothers and sisters of other Christian traditions and other faiths than Christianity. Although most of my colleagues in my own denomination have not openly challenged my position on other communions and other faiths, I have felt their uneasiness at the freedom with which I interact with persons of other faiths and the amount of time I have given to inter-church relationships and more recently, to inter-faith dialogue.

Very few of my denominational colleagues have taken time to find out from me why I give so much time and attention to relationships with persons outside of my own 'church' and outside of the 'household of faith', to use St. Paul's terminology. One does not have to be hypersensitive however, to detect apprehensiveness and unwillingness to 'journey' with me too far beyond the limits of ecclesiastical propriety.

When I accepted the offer of an appointment at the United Theological College of the West Indies (UTCWI) as the first holder of lectureship endowed by the Lutheran Church in America I wrote to the executive officer of my denomination asking for permission to accept the appointment. I got neither written nor verbal response to my letter from my colleague. However, I learned from a member of the committee that after much discussion it was agreed by the committee that I be allowed to accept. The same thing happened when I was asked by my colleagues to accept the appointment as President of the UTCWI. Although I was assured that I was the unanimous choice of members of the Board of Governors of the institution, I was never told by any of the officials of my denomination that I had their backing. Again I got no written reply to my request for leave to accept the appointment. What I heard from some of my older colleagues, was that the church would miss the pastoral skills honed over the thirty odd years since my ordination.

Because of what I view as the strange behavior of my colleagues toward my development as a servant of the church, I have found it difficult to resist the temptation to come to the conclusion that my fellow denominational leaders were unhappy about my decisions to accept not just non-pastoral but extra-denominational appointments. My feelings have been reinforced by the fact that my own denomination was the only one involved in the ownership of the UTCWI from which I got no gesture of affirmation at any time during my incumbency as Principal of the institution. In fact it was during my incumbency as President of the regional ministerial training institution that the decision was taken by my denomination to reduce its involvement in the use of resources of the college for the training of its leaders.

Since the termination of my full-time engagement with the United Theological College of the West Indies I have had the feeling of being kept on the margin of the life of the church in which I was cradled, nurtured and discipled. I have been left free to do whatever I choose to do and asked by the church to make contributions to its work in the world, only when others find it difficult to meet deadlines or have no interest in what I am asked to do, usually at very short notice.

In the light of my interpretation of my ritual of ordination and the implication of the same for personal growth, I usually take up the challenge of the assignment. I see each assignment as contributing to the building for the Kingdom of God in the context in which I live and serve, and for the empowerment of the people from whom I derive my ethno-political identity.

Marginalization by the leadership of my denomination has brought positive gains not only to me but also both to the church in particular and the world in general. The time not used in church activities has been available for research, writing, teaching, meditation and involvement in interfaith activities. I have had the time in retirement to explore a number of areas of concern with which I have been preoccupied for many years but have had little time to pursue because of pastoral and other ministerial involvement. Among these are the following:

a) The formation and empowerment of the Afro-Caribbean male especially

b) The liberation of the formerly colonized people of the Caribbean from all the lingering effects of the colonial and colonized mentality.

c) Forgiveness as necessity for personal liberation, personal and communal development as these relate to the achievement of authentic humanness and the unity of creation;

d) The removal of obstacles to healthy family life among the people of Jamaica, inappropriate approaches to family being one of the major causes of the persistence of underdevelopment, mis-development especially among Afro-Jamaicans.

e) The restoration of respect for traditional beliefs and values of non-European non-middle Eastern Peoples of the Caribbean, to the end that there may be diminution of excessive self-shame that is linked to ethno-historical origins and memories.

In the language of the late Paul Tournier, Austrian Psychiatrist, I have been saved by God from becoming the person of a 'place' I once occupied and set free to move on into places into which it is opportune for me to move.

I am now convinced that there is a positive correlation between meaningful growth as a person and being or feeling marginalized. Reflection on change in society and individuals, inevitably entails incurring the disgust, or even anger, of those close to you, and even having some denying their relationship with you when association with you is perceived to be dangerous. The truth is that it is normal and usual for persons to be wary of the consequences of taking on what is not only established but seemingly insurmountable.

Because of the fear of losing out in an attempt at changing the status quo, even those who stand most in need of change will resile from being seen to be identified with anyone who dares to take on the lion. Needless to say, this is why there have been many martyrs in history. It is safer to help build the tombs over the graves of those who dare to challenge the beast than to risk being torn to pieces by the beast.

What I keep discovering from time to time is that there are many secret supporters of the position I take from time to time in relation to issues of justice, with special reference to religious beliefs and affiliation, gender equality, the rights of minors and minority groups, and access to economic opportunity. Many who oppose those who take action or hesitate to be open in their support of them, have been known to join forces with them when it becomes less dangerous to do so. I have always been fascinated and encouraged by the parable of the seed growing secretly (Mark 4:26-29). What I have lived long enough to be convinced about is that God's will, in respect of justice, will eventually be manifestly done. What is interesting is how easily those who now support or even tolerate injustice, identify with the more desirable outcome of the struggle for radical change, when it is no longer risky to do so.

Following and Serving without Grudge or Fear

Throughout my life I have had the experience of being chosen to lead and this has happened even in circumstances in which I would have preferred not to be at the top of the line or in the chair. However, in most cases, those who have nominated me and voted for me have also been willing to assist, support and defend me even when in my own eyes I have not been deserving of any of this.

Those versed in the science of leadership may be able to offer plausible explanations for the leader-follower dynamics that apply to my case, but as far as I am concerned, it is certainly welcome and has given much satisfaction over the years since childhood but nevertheless remained a mystery to me. Certainly, concepts like 'charisma' do not apply to cases like mine. No one who is even barely discerning would consider someone like me charismatic. I cannot swear for what is said behind my back but I was in the sixth month of my seventeenth year that someone was heard by me to say that the 'presence' of someone like me among young Jamaicans does a great deal to make that national situation not completely hopeless at a time when young persons are bombarded with bad news about everything involving human beings.

My approach to leadership is something for which I must give credit to a number of persons and categories of persons whom I have been privileged to have as relatives, teachers, neighbours and colleagues throughout my life. Perhaps fortunately, I have had access to formal courses of study during my years of preparation for service in the Church and community. I am particularly grateful for what I learned about leading and following in courses taught by professors Bartholomew and Irion at Lancaster Seminary, Pennsylvania, in the early 1960's and Professors Adams, Hiltner, West and Emerson at Princeton Seminary in the late 1960's.

A significant feature of the learning experiences referred to was the opportunity offered to student –learners and teacher-learners to speak to and respond to each other in settings that were genuinely mutually respectful or open to giving and receiving criticism and commendation in the course of what was designated a 'lecture'. I remember a professor telling us how much he had learned from my responses at class sessions and papers I had written about features of the Jamaican or Caribbean socio-religious or pastoral contexts. I remember one of the professors named above, telling me how much I had helped him to overcome a psychological problem he had struggled with since he was a child. This was the case of a leader opening himself to being led by someone he had authority to lead by virtue of his status in the community of learners.

I have written the foregoing paragraphs as a prelude to my reporting on my experience of being a leader since the beginning period of my life referred to as 'retirement'. An experience that I have found rather interesting since the beginning of my retirement as a Minister in my denomination, is that of being introduced again and again as 'a former' one thing or another. In most settings in which I am introduced in relation to my service in the Christian ministry, I am referred to only as a former holder of an office of another. Occasionally I am asked to say what I do at the present time. When I tell of the things I do from day to day, year in year out, members of my audience ask what I mean by 'retirement' or why I refer to myself as being retired when I do so much from day to day. Some even refer to the need of Government and institutions like the church to do a review of the approach to retirement. Many are surprised when I disagree with them.

I disagree that retirement should begin when the working person is incapable of doing anything worthwhile or meaningful. In fact I go beyond disagreeing. I try to persuade younger colleagues to ensure that they are thoroughly prepared for retirement, proceed on their retirement when it becomes due, and spend the rest of their days doing as much as possible of what they wish and need to do but are not able to do before retirement. For this approach to retirement, I remain grateful to Professor James Emmerson of Princeton Seminary, who spoke a great deal (as he taught a course on developmental psychology) about fulfilling the need to be needed in the development period which follows what is referred to as 'retirement'.

It is out of my understanding of both the dynamics of servant leadership and the experience of having responsibility without designated authority, that I derive the sense of satisfaction I feel, in situations in which the bosses are not only younger colleagues but also former students. Nothing gives me greater pleasure than to be in a setting where as a part-time worker, I take orders from persons who are young enough to be children of children that I could have fathered in my mid-twenties! Again and again I tell my former students and younger colleagues, how much like old Simeon at the dedication of Jesus, I feel, when I find myself in settings in which they are now the leaders and I the follower.

Not only do I not feel resentment at being led by those whom I once led, I have a great deal of pride in the knowledge that I have had the good fortune of being a contributor to the making of current leadership. Many of the current leaders, who 'sat at my feet', in earlier times, will remember my telling them again and again, the need for those who currently prepare for leadership in any sphere of work, to be more knowledgeable and better prepared for the respective tasks than those who currently mentor them.

Those who now serve at any level should not only be free to hand over to younger colleagues or disciples, but also, to be qualified to earn the respect and gratitude of those who succeed or surpass them where they once held the reigns or occupied the place of authority and honour. Servant leadership as described by Jesus (Luke 22:24-30) is the ideal in any sphere of human relationship. Those who are not prepared to follow, do not deserve to be given the authority to lead or teach anywhere. Those who have led selflessly have no need to be fearful about following because they have been fulfilled through the experience of leading and need have no fear of losing either place or face. At the time of retirement those who have taught and led as a consequence of having learned and followed faithfully and conscientiously, should have the freedom to learn from others and both mentor and follow those who now teach and lead. The authority of the fulfilled retiree is in his/her character, wisdom and sense of security, not in continuing to have first or last word as to what is done, and how things are done, at the present time.

Unofficial 'Chaplain' to Many Families

A difficulty most pastors face is that of becoming completely detached from the families to which they became attached while serving in a parish especially when the tenure or period of service is lengthy. Needless to say, this perennial attachment is usually desired more by family than the ministerial incumbent and not welcomed to successors who invariably suspect the predecessor of interfering.

In every parish or 'charge' in which I have served there are families who expect me to share in every family event and are often not just disappointed but angry to the point where they will question your commitment to them.

A feature of this perennial tie with families is the practice, on the part of the older family members, of ensuring that the younger ones know that it was I who baptized them, married their parents, 'blessed' the family home or 'buried' a father, mother or some other relative. There are some families whose members are prepared to take up the tab for transportation and accommodation when the family event at which your participation is required is overseas or many miles away from your current residence.

There have been families who request that the favoured former pastor, pay a tribute or read the eulogy at the funeral or remembrance service. This can sometimes be awkward since one is expected to recall only laudable things about the deceased even in cases where there are facts about his/her life that would be known to members of the audience as anything but complimentary. In some cases, one puts one's reputation on the line, especially where the deceased is known for behavior that has left members of the community with bad memories.

Those who have served for extended periods in the same pastorate, cure, circuit or charge will easily identify with the situation descried above. If you are accepted and consequently regarded as part of that history of a community, rural, urban or suburban, you come to be regarded as part of the 'memory' of the community. Those members of the community who might be too young to recall any experience involving you physically, will be told about your contribution to the story of their people. In the language of African traditional religion, you become an 'ancestor' and therefore entitled to 'reverence'. In other words, you become for those people a member of the 'cloud of witnesses' which is a dimension of the 'world' of the people in certain places.

Those who share this experience because they have lived in or served communities in one capacity or another, will tell of the dangers of being available for special events long after you served a community. Present incumbents tend to be very sensitive to the attachment of predecessors to the people served by the latter. Those who are more secure in themselves, take it "in their stride", but there are those who are threatened by it to the point where they become openly critical of it and will even refuse to be present when a predecessor is a participant in an event. There have been cases in which the predecessor is asked to desist from accepting invitations to participate in events involving former parishioners. Needless to say, this is more easily said than done. In many cases successors shorten their tenure just to be away from the sphere in which their predecessor is still fondly remembered and revered.

There is no greater challenge to the integrity of pastors and officials of the church than that of dealing with the continuing relationship between former pastor and the families of the former parish and that between present incumbent and predecessor or predecessors with whom current parishioners find it difficult to break emotional ties. It requires a great deal of maturity and ethical sensitivity on the part of all concerned but especially on the part of pastoral colleagues. The wrong approach on the part of either predecessor or current incumbent can result in the rupturing of relationships between colleagues and between parishioner and either former pastor or present incumbent.

In my own case it is only in respect of one charge or pastorate that this matter has resulted in unhealthy relationships between myself and a successor. Of course, much has not been articulated but it has certainly been felt and observed by me and other, lay and ordained persons who know about the wisdom of not telling everything.

The ethical and other considerations apart, it has been my experience to have others treat me as one of their family's unofficial chaplains who is advised of all family events, painful or joyful, and consulted in times of crisis. Because of the persistence of some my own, and my own perception of the value of the relationship to these persons and the community as a whole, in most cases I have saved myself from carrying the burden of the consequences of unjustifiable excuses.

After all is said and done, it must be remembered that Ministers and priests are human beings who are capable of loving and being loved, befriending and being befriended by other human beings who just happen to be members or adherents of local church groups. Whilst therefore, we ought to guard against breaching codes of conduct we must be careful of degenerating into mere personages who are incapable of genuine 'I thou' relationships with fellow human beings. After all, the day must come for all of us when we must meet each other without our masks on and know each other as undeserving recipients of the grace of God.

To be numbered among the friends of families to which I have been privileged to be pastor is for me one of the great blessings of my life. For this I am deeply grateful not just to those whose hearts and homes are open to me but especially to Him who has bestowed on all of us the honour of identifying ourselves as members of His household. I cherish the privilege of being regarded as Minister by the families of the churches in the Lowe River Charge during the 1950's, those of the Retirement and Medina charges between 1955 and 1960, St Johns Presbyterian and then United between 1962 and 1973, Hope United between 1974 and 1981, St Paul's (Lockett Avenue) between 1990 and 1995. And, of course, the number of other congregations to which I have been interim pastor from time to time. To me there is no greater honour than that of being accepted by others as their spiritual leader.

On Being Ecumenically Human

I was first referred to as "The Ecumenical man" by the late Bela Vassady, Professor of Contemporary Theology, Lancaster Theological Seminary. This was in the academic year 1960-61 when I was an overseas student at the institution sponsored by the Evangelical and Reformed Church in the United States.

Professor Vassady had visited Jamaica during the late fifties and by his own admission was impressed by the freedom with which Jamaicans related to each other in respect of racial and religious differences. He not only sought me out for one to one conversations, he also asked the American students to talk with me as often as was possible. There were members of faculty who did the same, foremost among them Professor Al Bartholomew who taught a course on mission. I found at that institutions ready-made opportunity to look at the world with global human eyes rather than white American lenses.

Contrary to what many so-called conservative or fundamentalist Christians think, the term 'ecumenism' is not an invention of those they refer to as 'Liberal' or nominal Christians. Rather, it is derived from the words of Jesus used in what has come to be referred to as the missionary mandate. These words are recorded in the Gospel according to Matthew in the fourteenth verse of the twenty-fourth chapter and in the other passages such as Acts 11:28, 25:5. Romans 3:10, 16:14; et al.

Whilst being used popularly only in respect of Christian denominations or confessional traditions, the term actually has reference to all of humankind, including those human beings who have not even been exposed to Christian missionary or evangelistic activity.

Someone like myself could hardly be other than ecumenical in outlook. I grew up in a home with a Presbyterian mother and a Baptist father and later, had to live with young adult siblings belonging to the Seventh Day Adventist and Salvation Army traditions.

I married someone who was baptized and confirmed in the Anglican tradition and later belonged to the Christian Brethren tradition. Although baptized as a child in a Presbyterian Church as an adolescent making a commitment to the way of Christ in a Baptist Church in response to the preaching of a Baptist deacon-evangelist, I have had no difficulty worshipping with persons of other traditions. As the prophet Jonah learned after a bruising encounter between his theological misguided self and the immutably gracious God, I have been led to the firm conviction that salvation is indeed of God and not of nay theological or religious tradition (Jonah 2:9) as so many Christians think.

At the time of writing I am able to affirm with assurance that by the grace of God I am an ecumenical person using the work 'ecumenical' in an even wider sense than was intended by Professor Vassady to whom reference was made earlier. I feel a sense of affinity with all human beings of all religious and ethnic orientations. This is why it is not difficult for me to be part of the Inter-Faith movement and for those who may not be familiar with the interfaith movement, I need to state that it is a forum in which persons of different faiths affirm each other as human beings, respect each other's right to conceive of God as they do and feel a sense of responsibility to listen to others as they express their beliefs, and to defend the right of others to believe what they believe and practice their faith in such a manner that it does not obstruct others as they do the same.

As a follower of the teachings of Christ I believe that Christ belongs to the whole inhabited world despite the variety of ways in which persons conceive of God and salvation. Claims to possession of absolute faith are not only premature but contributory to the creation of barriers to healthy and meaningful communication between individuals and peoples of differing cultures and ethnic traditions. Claims to the possession of final truth do not presuppose the existence of the possibility of dialogue between protagonists of opposing views on any issue or point of view. In other words those who hold absolute views are not able to hear points of view that differ from theirs are not therefore able to accommodate the notion of plurality of approach to normative issues or matters related to faith and morality.

In my view, all religions are both means by which persons deal with issues of existence and salvation, and obstacles to the acquisition of reasonable understanding of God's will for the world and God's way of dealing with individuals and categories of persons indicated by the use of terms like 'race', 'religion', 'gender', 'nationality', and 'age'. Exclusivist approaches to religion have the same effect as discrimination based or any of the other categories referred to. Needless to say, most of the problems that now undermine desirable relationships all over the globe, have their roots in religious intolerance and the practice of excluding persons and curtailing their rights and freedoms. Unfortunately this applies to all of the major religions and the socioeconomic and political structures which these religions help to provide with sanctity and legitimacy.

Although being unequivocal about my own theological and moral convictions as a Christian, I am unequivocal about my support for the freedom of persons to pursue the religion or orientation or choice provided that in the pursuit of their own religion persons do not encroach on the freedom of those whose religious beliefs and practices differ from theirs. Of course, respect for the right to be religious in the way one chooses does not exclude the right of persons to seek to persuade others to accept the tenets of the religion they now follow as long as the former does not intrude on any of the freedoms of the latter.

The guiding principle of the involvement in ecumenical and interfaith relationships is that salvation is of God and not of any religion and God must not be confused with affirmations about God or Creedal statements and ritual practices. Neither must salvation be seen in terms of attachment to religious traditions and involvement in prescribed rituals. My faith makes me truly human and neither better than nor superior to human beings of other faiths or no faith at all. The essence of Christ-likeness is to be truly reconciled not only to God but also to all other human beings and the rest of God's creation. This ecumenism, and it is to this that God call us as bearers of the image of God. Because of the physical, social, economic, and religious characteristics of the context in which persons and peoples are socialized, they come to different conclusions about God, salvation, spiritually and personal and corporate destiny. However as we interface with fellow human beings in a multiplicity of contexts, we are challenged, first of all, to affirm, respect and listen to each other and hopefully, to learn from and work with each other in the making of a world in which we know each other as beneficiaries of the grace of God and grateful co-inhabitants of God's world.

The prophet Isaiah envisioned the ideal situation for all inhabitants of the world as one in which the lion and the lamb lie down together with neither being either desirous of devouring the other or fearful of being devoured. This situation is referred to as 'shalom' or a state of peaceful co-existence. In my view this is what salvation is all about and it is to this that Gods calls and leads by God's own spirit and through which we encounter God, albeit in a multiplicity of places and languages. Through the instrumentality of numbers of persons, of numbers of religious traditions, I have been led to this understanding of salvation and human destiny and I consider myself most fortunate at this time.

Working with Prime Minister Michael Manley

One of the decisions for which I got much flak for making was that of accepting the invitation to work as advisor to Michael Manley after the epoch, making elections of 1972. Of course what many persons did not know and may find it difficult to believe is that I accepted the Prime Minister's offer to serve with him only after consultation with leaders of my denomination and, that it was seen by them as part of the church's contribution to national development. Finally, I did not accept any reanimation even to cover the cost of travelling to Jamaica House or wherever else I had to meet the Prime Minister and government technocrats when my presence was needed.

What I learned from Christians from time to time about involvement with the Prime Minister led me to two conclusions which after over thirty years, I have not been persuaded to change.

First of all, most of those who spoke with me were of the view that the affairs of state were perceived by many as unrelated to the vocation and responsibility of the person designated for pastoral work. What politicians or legislators do is regarded by many Christians as 'worldly', outside of the 'realm of redemption', or the saving of souls. If it is that in which followers of Christ get involved incidentally whilst they are 'in the flesh' but certainly, not something that is worthy of the attention of those who are committed to the preparation of the elect for the hereafter. To those who see the world as outside of the realm of redemption, involvement on matters of state must be left to the 'people of the world'. Needless to say, this view of politics has derived from a misinterpretation of what is reported in the gospel according to John (18:36) as the response of Jesus to those or his disciples who wanted to respond physically to their master's assailants on the eve of his arrest, trial and crucifixion. This is an interpretation which has led to much of the worldly pessimism on the part of the followers of the way of Christ, and, by extension, the less than responsible approach of religious enthusiast to the evils that persist in most societies in the realms of politics and economics. To those with that view, God has abandoned part of the world to those who are opposed to the claims of the kingdom as interpreted in the light of the teaching of Christ in what is referred to as the Sermon on the Mount as recorded in chapters five through seven of the Gospel According to Matthew.

Needless to say, this contradicts notions of the indiscriminate love of neighbours and the sovereignty of God the Creator over all of creation.

Other fellow Christians and religiously indifferent fellow-citizens who objected to my working with Prime Minister Manley did so for party political reasons. They saw the association of a leader of the church with the leader of a political party other than the one supported by them, as giving an advantage to their opponents. In the political climate of the day, they saw me not so much as an insincere Christian as someone who is not expected to be impartial using his/her influence in the interest of some, to the detriment of others.

Both of the perspectives on my involvement with a political leader are due to the need for a more mature approach to civic responsibility. Students of Christian ethics view this as evidence of the need for raising of awareness, with special reference to the practice of disinterested or 'neighbor regarding' love as illustrated by Jesus in parables like those of the Good Samaritan recorded in the tenth chapter of Luke and that of the Sheep and the Goats, recorded in the twenty-fifth chapter of the Gospel of Matthew.

Another reason many persons took offence or were puzzled by my involvement with Michael Manley's 'politics of change', is that as a consequence of many decades of exposure to what some refer to as 'Missionary Theology', most Christians have come to view the injustices especially of a colonial and post-colonial situation like Jamaica, as 'ordained' by God and therefore, not open even to gradual change. Some even see the victims of the unjust situations as deserving of the hardships they suffer because of the sins of their fore parents. Those who hold that view see attempts at political and economic transformations as 'flying into God's face' or trying to force God's hands. It is no wonder therefore that beneficiaries of the social and economic status quo, in situations like some in the United States of America, encourage theological fundamentalism or conservatism. They know that that understanding of God's involvement in the world facilitates the persistence of injustice, and consequently, the perpetuation of inequalities in the distribution of economic opportunity. Happily for Jamaica the theological climate has changed considerably since the 1970s and many who objected to the involvement of persons like myself in the politics of change of the day, now involve unapologetically in what I would refer to as instrumentation of disinterested love as illustrated by Christ in many of the parables recorded in the Gospels.

In my view, Michael Manley was a person whose mission was not yet understood even by the majority of those who stood to gain from it. He had a more realistic view of the teachings of Christ than many of those who use religious language where he used the language of political and social realism.

As in most cases of impending change, those who feel threatened usually resort to 'scaremongering' tactics. This means that they find ways of persuading the more credulous who are both more numerous and the ones most likely to benefit from change.

As many of his erstwhile opponents have come to admit to Michael Manley's being both idealist and impatient, underestimated the enormity of the apprehensiveness of the upper middle class and the depth of the ignorance of the disinterested majority as to what is in their best interest.

What was surprising to my colleague the Reverend Sam Reid and me was Manley's sensitivity to the plight of the poor people of Jamaica.

In addition to being very accessible especially to the poor children of the inner city, a fact to which I am able to testify as a pastor to inner city communities, Prime Minister Manley was prepared to commit his comparatively meager resources to the upliftment of people who were chronically deprived. The following story is testimony to this.

When the basic salary of the Prime Minister was increased from eighteen thousand to twenty- two thousand dollars per month, the Prime Minister reported to some of his advisors that he would put four thousand dollars monthly into a fund to be applied to the provision of educational opportunity for poor children of Central Kingston, the constituency he represented in parliament. In my hearing two of his advisors reminded him that he needed to think of his own children for whose education he was responsible as a father. He was adamant about making a sacrifice for the most needy, insisting that his own children would be adequately provided for. My respect for him increased considerably.

I was convinced about Michael Manley's abhorrence of the persistence in Jamaica of discrimination on the basis of class and skin colour. Whatever doubt I may have had about his commitment to changing this situation, was completely removed as a consequence of the responses he gave to an issue which arose on the eve of the General Elections of 1976.

Two highly placed supporters of his party requested my presence at a meeting with him as party leader. At the meeting they would try to persuade him to give endorsement to a move to change the candidate for one of the constituencies of the parish of Manchester. These two leaders, one a medical practitioner and the other an educator, after expressing their admiration for the qualification and character of their candidate, asked that he be requested to give place to another of lighter complexion since the electors of that constituency have never returned as a member of parliament any person who would be considered as 'flag black'.

Party leader Michael Manley became furious. He told the petitioners that had the Reverend gentleman not been present he would have used very strong language to them for asking him to be a party to anything of that sort. He declared that he was prepared to see his party lose in that constituency rather than betray his late father the founder of the party he was leading, by acceding to a request to select a prospective member of the nation's Parliament on the basis of the colour of his/her skin. The candidate in question lost the election but Michael Manley won a significant moral victory in the estimation of principled people.

Michael Manley was keen on doing right, especially by unprivileged people of our country on the development issues such as Land Reform, access to economic opportunity and the removal of impediments to advancement at the workplace in all areas of national life.

With respect to religion, Michael Manley while savoring his Methodist background, insisted on government's religious neutrality or the retention of a situation in which no person be favored for the appointment or denied opportunity for advancement in the society, on the basis of religious beliefs or affiliation.

For reasons which I was not able to ascertain, Prime Minister Manley was interested in the views and teaching of Thomas Aquinas the epoch-making Roman Catholic theologian of the thirteenth century. He was very keen on knowing what Aquinas had to say on a number of ethical and political questions on which the Vatican gave directions to the faithful from time to time.

An assignment that I will long remember in respect of my work with Michael Manley is that of providing the major theological ingredients for the Jamaica Prime Ministers keynote address to the World Council of Churches General Assembly in Nairobi, Kenya in the summer of 1972. I will not forget the experience of working with persons like anthropologist M.G. Smith, novelist John Hearne, Anglican theologian Ernle Gordon and the Prime Minister himself. After many days of hard work sometimes punctuated with strong words and violent disagreement, we hammered out a document which from reports received by me from overseas scholars and church leaders, was very well received. I remember being hugged by a Danish Theologian in a meeting in Detroit, Michigan, where I was being prepared for involvement in an ecumenical pastors programme sponsored by the Presbyterian Church in the United States. Once this lady heard the word 'Jamaica' she came across to where I was, asked if I knew Prime Minister Michael Manley and proceeded to tell the audience that the Prime Minister of my country was not only the most handsome of the presenters at the international event, but also, the smartest. Needless to say I felt proud to be a Jamaican and to have made a small contribution to the making of the document that earned my country the accolades that were so generously being heaped upon it.

Michael Manley was by no means a man without flaws and shortcomings. In fact his sins are well known to both friends and foes of his day. Again, he knew how to be ready to exclude himself from discussions on issues dealing with subjects like family life because according to him he had no credibility in those areas. However in the view of many like myself who had opportunity to interface with him, he was not necessarily more sinful than the rest of us but rather, more ready to confess his sins to others, rather than being pretentious about personal virtues.

As has been the case of those before and after him who have dared to lead the changes against social ills, that make victims of the majority, he incurred the wrath, even of good people and faithful supporters of his own party.

Speaking of persons of the late Prime Minister's own party, not many Manley watchers know of the difficulty he had in getting his supporters to appreciate the fact that once appointed to Parliament, legislators have more responsibility to be completely unbiased in the service of their fellow citizens. I recall being called to intervene in an issue involving Prime Minister Manley and an enthusiastic party worker who protested the appointment of a former member of Parliament (for the opposition) to an administrative position in one of the government agencies. I got involved in the matter because the "comrade" involved was a member of my congregation who asked me to take up the matter with her party leader. Prime Minister Manley's response to her was that first of all, he had no intention of interfering with the decisions made by heads of agencies and government departments, and secondly the person whose appointment. My parishioner was furious at first, about the response from her leader but soon came to appreciate the principled position he had taken on the matter.

An interesting thing about Mr. Manley's relationship with the person whose approach was questioned by the party supporter is that when the person was hospitalized in critical condition he got to her bedside before any of the senior leaders of her own party.

In my view, Michael Manley with all his shortcomings, was a very civilized human being who showed compassion and magnanimity that many do not expect of those involved in the cut and thrust of competitive politics. His approach to his opponents and critics epitomized American politician Bob Dole's quip during a convention of his own party, that the person on the opposite side was his political opponent not his enemy. I remain convinced that all the late leader set out to do needed to be done in his time and much is yet to be done. The problem with him is not that he forgot the experiences of his counterparts in history like Moses, Marcus Garvey, Mahatma Gandhi, Martin Luther King, to name only a few, but that in many cases they expected too much of their fellowmen. In the final analysis however, what needs to be done has to be done and eventually gets done although not in the lifetime of the conceptualiser or initiator, or, for that matter, according to the original vision.

In the words of Jesus, the Christ who Himself was misunderstood, opposed and condemned for advocating radical change in the prevailing status quo; the people often kill the prophets then erect elaborate monuments over their graves when they (the people) come to appreciate the meaning of the prophet's message.

On reflection on what transpired in Jamaica in respect of the mission and approach of Michael Manley, I am convinced that what was envisaged had to be attempted, and eventually achieved. I therefore consider myself fortunate to have been privileged to be asked to help my compatriots to understand the politics of a great Jamaican leader, who like many of his kind in history was indeed more than his detractors made him out to be.

Some Defining Moments Remembered

In everybody's pilgrimage from the dawn of self-consciousness to the then end of self-awareness there are epochal events which give meaning to one's personal history. Unfortunately for many persons in all cultures or social contexts, many of these events do not get recalled because in the memory of the individual and his/her family these events are associated with shame, guilt, remorse or pain. This is a great pity as exponents of contemporary psycho-analysis would say, because it is in the recalling of these events that one experiences personal liberation and self-fulfillment.

Of course, in everyone's lifetime there are several of these memorable moments and therefore, in the short story of a long life, only the most significant can be recorded.

At the age of six I was challenged to figure out the process leading to the advent in the world, of a new person or family member. My younger brother Lewis was born at home with the assistance of my maternal grandmother who was one of the local 'nannys'. The morning after, I heard the cry of the new intruder into my domain and asked my father how the young one got into our space. He told me some mythical story about the baby being brought here by a big bird from wherever he was.

When I shared the story with a slightly older but more worldly wise schoolmate at infant school, I was told by him what happens from the beginning of the whole process to the time when the nanny slaps the new born gently to get it to announce its arrival. When I shared with my father what my worldly wise fellow toddler told me, he admonished me about walking to school with that boy. I now know that he was annoyed that he had allowed a little six year old to preempt him in an area in which he would have been expected to give leadership to his six year old.

The shape of my left index finger is a perennial reminder to me and older members of my family, of the day when it was all but completely severed from the rest of my youthful body. The accident necessitated my having to be a patient in the Savanna-la-mar public hospital for nearly three weeks.

At the early age I had opportunity to learn a few useful lessons about illness and the behaviour of persons in the case of health professionals. I also learned a little about my own identity as a member of the local community and fledgling member of the wider community. Needless to say, I got much attention from hospital staff, older patients and family members.

I owe much of what I have become to that experience. It could have contributed to my interest in the acquisition of pastoral skills and the pastoral outlook in general. Throughout my life, the disfigured finger has kept me reminded of that crisis. As an older boy growing up in the local community and school I was one day persuaded by some of less 'protected' schoolmates to go with them on an unauthorized trip that took us quite a distance from the school. Returning to the school long after we were expected to I was confronted by an angry Principal who told me how much I had let down not just himself but the school community and the whole district. Someone like myself, he said, was expected to lead and not follow.

I felt ashamed of my behavior but what happened to me then, helped to confirm in me a sense of being a leader not only of my peers but also of the older folk in the local community. My father's reprimand which came later than the Principal's on the same day, served to reinforce my sense of being a leader.

As a ministerial student, it was a defining moment for me, when as a member of the student body of the smaller of the three non-Anglican colleges; I was elected president of the group. I had difficulty figuring out why I was chosen over colleagues who were much more urbane than I and had better scholastic records. What happened later in my career in respect of leadership led me to conclude that one does not necessarily have to resort to lobbying as a means of getting elected or appointed to positions of leadership. I also became convinced about the pointlessness of trying to discover why some are chosen over their peers in one context or another. Since mid-teens it has been my policy not to seek office and to leave before having to be persuaded to do so.

I got one of the big surprises of my life when I was told in the fall of 1968 by the General Secretary of the United Church, the Reverend Clement Thomas, that I was the nominee of a majority of the Area Councils of the United Church in Jamaica and the Grand Cayman for the Moderator's chair during the calendar year 1969-70. I had not yet had my fortieth birthday and felt a little diffident about taking on the challenge. However with the assurance of the support of many of my peers in the ministry and a host of lay leaders, I accepted. For reasons better known by those responsible for proposing my reelection for two consecutive terms, I ended up being the first person in the history of my denomination to serve three terms consecutively. For my sins I was elected to another one year term a decade after the conclusion of the third year of my first incumbency.

I recall as a defining moment that time when as I sat in a meeting of the Executive of the Jamaica Council of Churches, the illustrious Chairman of the Jamaica District of the Methodist Church, the Rev. Dr. Hugh Sherlock, tapped me gently on my shoulder and said in a quiet but serious tone "I hope you are preparing to take over as the next President of the Council!". Out of my sense of reverence for someone of Father Sherlock's stature in church and nation, I was scared to tell him that he could not be serious. What followed almost immediately after the patriarch's gentle challenge is now part of the history of the church in Jamaica.

Among other things, the period 1969-71 marked the era in global politics when the ideological battle lines were clearly drawn, challenging not only dependent Third World countries but also the established Christian church to assert their right to choose their own ideological path and above everything else become the mediator between the two contending blocs on the geo-political arena. It was during this time that the voices of the erstwhile dependent churches of the Third World found expression in what have become known as Third World Theologies, what is referred to as Caribbean Theology being one of these.

My leadership of Jamaica Council of Churches therefore coincided with the occurrence of dramatic changes in the perception of the role of the Christian church in the social, economic and political development in Jamaica and the rest of the English speaking Caribbean, with special reference to change and the management of change.

During the period between the late sixties and the beginning of the eighties, there was a proliferation of philosophical discussion throughout the Caribbean region which was manifestation of the increase in awareness among erstwhile colonial subjects and other disenfranchised categories of people throughout the world. A significant aspect of this was the insistence of the current leadership in many churches that there should be a theological dimension of what was indeed a revolution. Understandably, there was cleavage between the more cautious leaders of the churches and the so-called radicals. As was the case in the United States perhaps out of the fear of losing the material support which comes from those who perceive the Judeo-Christian scriptures as being identical with the 'infallible word of God' and therefore not open to intellectual challenge or change of interpretation in any age or context. That situation changed gradually as interaction between representatives of both camps increased especially in response in initiatives taken by leaders of the so-called liberal wing of the church. It was during that period that contacts increased and greater collaboration took place between the leaders of the more conservative 'Churches' and the Jamaica Council of Churches became, in what are now referred to as umbrella groups. Ironically these were mysteriously driven more close together by the ravaged of Hurricane Gilbert which Struck Jamaica in August 1988. It was also during the period 1969-72 that the Roman Catholics became members of the Jamaican Council of Churches and Anglicans returned to it after a number of years during which time they were out because the reluctance of a former bishop to affirm the ecclesiastical authenticity of one of the nontraditional member churches of the Council, the churches of God in Jamaica. Incidentally, the Church of God in Jamaica withdrew from membership in the council when the Anglicans were re-admitted citing their uneasiness about working with those who 'dissed' them in a previous dispensation.

My activist approach to the leadership of the Jamaica Council of Churches brought me into conflict with members of the more conservative wing of the churches. These Christians colleagues were not yet ready for the new era of Christian witness in which spokespersons for the church, out of their understanding of the notion of the sovereignty of God over all creation, felt that it was imperative for them to take on the political and economic structures in the interest of those who are victims of the practice of injustice against those least able to defend themselves and their kind against the beneficiaries of compromised interpretation of the law of love as it was articulated by Jesus according to the Witness of the writers of the Gospels.

The invitation by the President of the United Theological College of the West Indies marked the beginning of my involvement in the writing of Christian theology. Writing an article on the challenge of the Rural Church was for me the fulfillment of the Wish of President Harry Richardson of the Interdenominational Theological Centre, Atlanta, Georgia, who after reading a paper presented to him at the end of the course taught by himself, observed that I might consider writing as a hobby or vocation. I needed only the kind of responses I got to an article in Caribbean Journal of Religious Studies to assure me that the time had arrived for confirmation of that mentors prophetic perception of my endowment in the area of literacy production. Thanks to president Richardson and my colleagues, Horace Russel and William Watty, my publisher, Dr. Val Chamber and more recently Dr.Theresa Lowe-Ching of St. Michael's Theological College and Centre for Caribbean Spirituality, (Roman Catholic), among others. My gifts as a writer have been amply affirmed through the responses to what they and others have challenged me to produce as instruments for the prosecution of the ministry of Christ in my life.

Today, like Black American Theologian James Cone, I am one of those who are of the view that at whatever is considered satisfactory by a group a of students in a formal setting or audience made up of conscientious listeners, is worth being considered for publication in the interest of advancement of human society at every level.

Becoming the unanimous choice as President of the United Theological College of the West Indies is another event in my life that is indelibly etched in my memory. As is at in a meeting of the Board of Governors sometime in 1985, the late Reverend Caleb Cousins, a former Chairman of the Jamaica District of the Methodist Church and Methodist Warden at the college, drew close to me and said softly in his characteristically humorous manner, 'I hope you are preparing to take on the challenge". He was not prepared to entertain any discussion with me as to why it should be someone else and not I. An interesting feature of the process leading up to the installation in that office was that even though they would have nominated me, no member of the executive of my own denomination even asked me if I had any interest in taking on the challenges of that appointment.

The invitation by the British Council of Churches to be part of a term of theological educators from Commonwealth countries including Great Britain, to observe approaches to ministerial training in that country, and recommend changes where these were deemed to be necessary, was for me a high point in my career and I was elated when one of my British hosts advised me that my report which was the first submitted, would be used as the model for those who had not yet completed theirs. My sense of satisfaction in relation to the exercise to, was confirmed when I was told by a member of the faculty of one of the British Theological colleges that most of the recommendations made by the Commonwealth team were implemented by a large number of the institutions just about a year after they were submitted. Among other things, it left me with the conviction that despite the paucity of our resources we are doing something worthwhile at the regional ecumenical centre for ministerial formation.

A moment in my life that has contributed in no small way to my development as a person and leader came with the announcement that a request of his window the Hon. Mrs. Edna Manley, I was the person to be asked to preach at the first of the funeral services to be held for the late National Hero Norman Washington Manley. That service was held at the Porus Methodist church chapel where the National Hero was baptized as child over seventy years before. The challenge to prepare an appropriate message for that service has been one of the defining moments of my life. Subsequent to that it has been my privilege to be the preacher at the first memorial service for the National Hero and at the centennial of his birth some time later.

As the chief executive officer of the Ecumenical institution, the United Theological College of the West Indies, I had some memorable experiences. Just a month before the occurrence of Hurricane Gilbert 1988, I took it upon myself to accept the advice of our insurers to have a revaluation of our insured assets done, with a view to increasing the premium. The value arrived at was eleven times the current one. Before meeting of the Finance and General Purpose Committee I went ahead and paid the premium in accordance with the valuation. The hurricane devasted the building of the college, but providentially, we were adequately covered and so be awarded over a thousand percent of what we would be entitled to under the old valuation. A member of the board of governors who rebuked me for preempting the board was challenged by other members who commended me for having the foresight to do what I did. I had saved the Churches hundreds of thousands of dollars which they would have had to find to take care of rehabilitation work on their respective properties. In fairness to my chief detractor though, I must report that I received a verbal apology from him just weeks after he questioned the propriety of my action in the matter.

Among the lessons learned from the scenario reported above are, first of all, that enslavement to the letter of the law, regulation or tradition, can shackle an institution, business or community; and that a manager or leader should exercise the freedom to do what is in the best interest of the group or enterprise led by him/her, as long as the decision to act is based on sound judgment made on the careful assessment of the realities and possibilities perceived at the time of a particular decision.

Because of the significance of race and colour in human relationships, I consider it necessary to recall something that happened to us just about three days before our departure from Northern Ireland at the end of July 1973. Winifred and I had heard much about the city of Donegal and decided to do a tour of this beautiful place before returning home. At about a quarter of two o'clock we went into a restaurant and proceeded to order lunch. To our astonishment, we were told they were not serving lunch at that time. Determined to ascertain whether or not it was a case of racial discrimination, we decided to ask whether there was anything they could serve us at this time because we were so hungry. We were rather relieved when we were told that we could get sandwiches and coffee, tea or fruit juice, and informed that at that restaurant they served lunch until one thirty in the afternoon. We were able to leave the Emerald Isle with the assurance that we had not been discriminated against on the basis of race or colour.

Among the lessons I learned as a follower of the teachings of Christ, is that of the danger of rushing to judgment too hastily, especially in intercultural issues. Again, because of my international experience in Ireland I have since become more capable of contributing to the ministry of reconciliation, especially in as it relates to the subject of religion and race. Since my stint in Northern Ireland, I have lived with the conviction that the other person is never a race, religion, class or gender and that in spite of his/her identity in respect of any of these categorized, is a sister or brother with whom to me, it is always an experience of the grace of God.

Those who are aware of the importance of family relationships to making of persons will appreciate the inclusion in my life story of this story. My wife Winifred decided sometime in the 1970s to take a year off to complete requirements for a master's degree in education. She proceeded to a university in Florida because of the proximity of the campus to the residence of a sister who resided in that part of the world. At the end of the first week away she called to say that she had decided to cancel the arrangement to acquire the advanced status away from home. She thought of the difficulties I might experience in caring for our three young children and the possible ultimate consequences for our marriage and the development of the children. On returning home she made arrangements to purse her advanced degree at the University of the West Indies so that she would be at home and therefore accessible to the children and myself. Everything worked out beautifully for all us and indeed for countless number of persons who are beneficiaries of our contribution to the many years of national life in which we have been involved. It is well known through the research carried out by students of family life and developmental psychology how much the prolonged absence of a parent can disturb the social and emotional development of persons in the earlier years of life.

In the post-retirement years of my career, I have been blessed by opportunities to teach courses dealing with African traditional religions, African Retentions and the Caribbean and Third World Liberation Theologies, at both undergraduate and graduate levels, at the University of the West Indies and the United Theological College of the West Indies.

The experience of preparing course outlines and lectures for these courses, interacting with students from across the Caribbean and occasionally from Northern America and African Continent itself, has contributed immensely to my intellectual development and spiritual enrichment. The more I reflect on what I learn about African patterns of spiritualities the more appreciative I become of the dynamics of many of the problems that beset the descendants of victims of colonial domination and missionary theologies. I am convinced, however, that despite what has been done wrong throughout the history of Christendom all is not lost for the successors of both the perpetrators and the victims, and there are endless possibilities for all of humankind through the discovery of the treasures of the spiritualities of peoples of the underside of history.

So much of what I regard as the defining moments in my life has occurred through the instrumentality of leaders of the Presbyterian Church in the United States. In addition to opportunities for formal study and research leading to the achievement of academic honors, Presbyterians (who would be dubbed 'liberal' by the more conservative Christian groups) have allowed me to partner with them in some crucial and even controversial initiatives aimed at effecting change in the perspective of Americans on the rest of the world, with special reference to the involvement of the American government and American business in the Western Hemisphere.

During the late 1970s I was part of a commission appointed by the Presbyterian Church to examine some of the issues involved in the American approach to the Fidel Castro regime in Cuba. That experience provided me with opportunity to listen to the views of American citizens on Cuba that did not coincide with the official approach to the revolutionary approach of President Fidel Castro. It was interesting to hear Cubans living in the United States explain their presence as students in the United State even though supportive of the Castro regime.

Another involvement with the leadership of the Presbyterian Church in the United States that I consider significant, had reference to the invasion of the island of Grenada following the assassination of the country's revolutionary leader Maurice Bishop and his colleagues in 1983. Having heard of my role with the drafting of a response to the crisis issued by my own church, the United Church in Jamaica and the Cayman Islands, officials of the Presbyterian Church, USA, invited me to join them at a meeting in Atlanta Georgia where they would be involved in drafting their response as a church to what the Reagan government had done to the small island with a population of less than a hundred thousand people. If I had any doubts before, that event about the respect that our powerful neighbours to the north had for the leaders of the Caribbean, it was all dispelled after my involvement with my fellow Christians of that powerful empire. Needless to say, the powerful statement issued by my own church of less than twenty thousand members, formed the nucleus of the statement issued by our much later and much more powerful sister church. Among other things, my understanding of St. Paul's exposition of the concept of the complementarities of the value of gifts of the church (1 Corinthians 12) became much more meaningful to me. So also, the concept of the Catholicity of the Church, a concept which dominates the scriptures of the New Testament.

Among the moments that I treasure as an ecumenical person are those in which I had the great privilege of sitting at table in a restaurant on Bechwith Street, Atlanta, Georgia, with the celebrated twentieth century prophet and martyr Martin Luther King Jnr. It was during the academic year 1961-62 and I was a graduate student and research assistant to the Professor of Religion and Society at the Interdenominational Theological Centre which is part of the Atlanta University Center. 'M.L.K.' as we called him, having learned that I was from Jamaica was eager to talk with me about Norman Manley who was later declared National Hero; we spoke of his admiration for Norman Manley of Jamaica and Pandit Nehru the Prime Minister of India. It was a great privilege to be living in Atlanta in those days for among other things I could go to hear Martin Luther King Snr., and elsewhere in the city where he addressed audiences from time to time on the need for the liberation of the people of the United States of America.

In less than 15 years after returning home from Atlanta, I was to become involved with another set of Presbyterian leaders in the United States. This time it was the faculty and students of the Columbia Theological Seminary which in the early sixties was an integral part of racially segregated 'South'. Like my friends George and Lois McCredie of York Pennsylvania who dared to allow me to take their infant son David into my arms and baptize him in the presence of a 'lily white' American congregation, Professor Erskine Clarke on behalf of Columbia Seminary community entrusted me with the supervision of white American ministerial students the summer of 1979. The transaction was to be nucleus of ventures in Theological education and ministerial formation involving five theological seminaries in the South and the United Theological College of the West Indies, Mona, to begin with and afterwards to include the Codrington College of Barbados and the Cave Hill campus of the University of the West Indies.

The Doctor of Ministry programme which grew out of the collaboration to the enhancement of ecumenical relationships between so-called traditional churches and churches of the non-traditional umbrella groups of churches in Jamaica, who, prior to the 1980s saw the ecumenical ministerial training institutions as liberal institutions with which they hesitated to entrust the training of ministers

The arrangement which brought the American Theological institutions in partnership with the United Theological College was later to become a significant global one. In the later 1980s, American and Caribbean students were joined by students drawn from churches of the Council for World Mission, an intra- confessional ecclesiastical agency which facilitates collaboration by churches which were formerly related to the London Missionary Society through which the congregational church in England and Wales reached out to places on the Continent of Asia, Africa, the islands in the Pacific and the British Caribbean. The Training in Mission (T.I.M.) programmed brought together members of churches in the former British territories on the continent of Africa, India, Hong Kong, Sri Lanka, Bangladesh, the Netherlands, the islands of the Pacific and the British territories in the Caribbean and South America. The coming together of peoples from the Americas, Europe, Asia, the Pacific and Southern Africa provided opportunities for international, multi-cultural and inter-racial interaction and co-existence which should be brought to the attention of both ecclesiastical and secular historians. Among other things, this intermingling of persons from so many racial cultural and religious backgrounds, has exposed the world to new dimensions of relationships that should serve to nullify the effects of the arrogant approaches to inter-national relationships and even ecumenical relationships in which the agenda is set by rich and powerful and the interactions staged and contained by those who sponsor these transactions.

My moments of discovery, empowerment and transformation have come through the agency of thousands of persons throughout life, but there are some whom I feel compelled to include even at the risk of being condemned by many who desire not to be referred to. Many of these persons have been little children, some precocious or inquisitive, adolescents, very many men and women who have been my pupils in primary and secondary schools, universities, and theological colleges. Needless to say, thousands have been persons who fall into category of 'man in the street' or person into whose company you just happen to find yourself from time to time.

How can I forget the lady from a Moravian congregation in Kingston who once remarked that leaders of the churches in Jamaica need to come to understand earlier than later that 'pickney church can't lead grown up nation'. This lady is just one of the many who would have yearned for space in which she could speak and be assured of being heard and taken seriously. Unfortunately, in the kind of world in which she has been unfortunate enough to have been born, very few like herself would have had opportunity to contribute to the store of knowledge which should be part of the identity of full affirmed part of the family of God's people. It should make a world of difference to such persons if those who are named and heard by significant others from time to time, would by some meaningful gesture, affirm their humanity the way many have done to me. There would be less pain in the experience of people in our world and less cause for feelings of guilt and shame.

I am grateful for the freedom to acknowledge my indebtedness to the many who have contributed in one way or another to what I am and what I hope will be remembered as my contribution to the enrichment to human experience in the world.

Among other things, I am indebted to god and the countless numbers of persons in various circumstances who have helped me to acquire the ability to hear and respond realistically and creatively to what I hear and believe. It is this, more than anything else that has enabled me to do what I have been able to do in the course of my pilgrimage from the dawn of my elf-consciousness to the point of my current state of self-awareness and spiritual maturity.

What some refer to as defining moments, come in great numbers and with varying degrees of frequency, in the life span of every human being. They are what writers like William Shakespeare refer to as the 'current that serves' and in the scriptures of the New testament as the 'Kairos' or opportune moments, or, that time in the life of a person, community or nation, when something happens that determines the course of the history of the individual and the community from that moment onward. The moment in my own life to which reference has been made herein, are just a few of the many that deserve to be recorded, but those are mentioned because of this writers' perception of their relevance to this version of his story. Some readers of this story might want to recall some of these in reconstructing the memories of their encounter with the writer in some of the events of which his story is comprised.

Some Blessings of Retirement

One of the more cherished blessings of the time of retirement is the freedom of the retiree to spend quality time with spouse, children, grandchildren and members of extended families when one is fortunate to have these categories of persons around. Of course, for this to be optimally true and realizable there need to be means of bare necessities of life and a few luxuries like books, newspapers, periodicals, occasional trips abroad and weekends away from home.

Owing largely to my wife's genius as a manager of resources we have not been the poorest of low pension retirees. Despite the pittance both of us get as pensioners after working for the Ministry of Education and the Church respectively, we are not condemned to worrying about paying utility bills and taxes and procuring food and other vital necessities of life.

Because Winnifred chose to put her savings into real estate, she has been a landlady who has been very fortunate with the tenants she has had. She has therefore been able to use her time to do gardening around the house, giving leadership in neighbourhood organizations and participating vigorously in activities of the Church and Alumni association and taking care of siblings. I on the other hand, in order not to deplete my small savings too early, have used most of my time lecturing in areas of my competence in a number of educational institutions, the UWI, ITLD, an affiliate of the United Church in Jamaica and the Cayman Islands, and the UTCWI. What is most fulfilling to me are the opportunities and time I have to work with leaders and prospective leaders in church and wider society, as they prepare themselves for other levels of engagement with the constituencies of churches and the wider society. For my sins I have been entrusted by my academic colleagues with the responsibility of accompanying graduate students in various areas of the theological enterprise in their search for answers to the questions being raised about reality, in language about God, language referred to as 'theology'.

I find very few activities as challenging as those related to the mentoring of students in tertiary institutions especially in the study of religion and the behavior of religious persons and the concerns of persons and groups about questions of 'ultimate concern'. Among other things, it challenges one to remain alert and aware of what is taking place in academia and wherever else persons and groups wrestle with existential, relational and theological questions.

Contrary to what many think, retirement is not the time to wind down, and become invisible in preparation for final demise. It is indeed not only an inevitable phase of the life of the individual but also a significant stage in the life of a person. I looked forward to retirement as a stage of my own development when I could have time to do many of the things I thought of earlier in life but had neither the time nor the resources to deal with. Of course, it is of utmost importance that one is prepared as thoroughly as possible and that preparation has reference not just to personal savings but also to physical and mental health and attitude.

It is important for the enjoyment of retirement how one views one's self as a person and part of the total scheme of things in one's world and during one's lifespan. In one of the courses I pursued as a post graduate student much emphasis was placed on the 'need to be needed'. Retirees become preoccupied with dying not because of their years of life or their inability to do the things they did easily in midlife, but mainly because they are not convinced that they are able to contribute anything to the common good. Many retirees are doubtful at all times, despite what is said by way of commendation in response to what they do, that what they are asked to do is really needed or appreciated.

It is out of this nagging sense of doubt, and by extension, self-worth, that many retirees become so preoccupied with physical appearance, memory and the sincerity of those who express appreciation for what they do or say. Needless to say, this attitude to themselves contributes to the actualization of what they fear and dread. The more they worry, the more justifiable their worries become and the stronger the wish to enter into their rest.

In my case, one of the challenges is to find the time to do the things one is required and requested to do and get to places one is invited to go. Again and again former students express the view that I look much younger than I did five years before I gave up the Presidency of the UTCWI, when I had exactly four years of service left before retirement at the age of sixty-five. A former parishioner in my last pastoral charge once jokingly remarked that the reason I looked younger in retirement was that I no longer had to deal with what she referred to as the 'hauling and pulling' of parishioners.

Opportunities for self-development and service in retirement have come in abundance and for this I am grateful not only to those with whom I interact, but also to my mentors especially during postgraduate study and those who have taught me through the printed page, writers like Paul Tournier the late Swiss Psychiatrist and author who more than many others did much to help readers to explore and appreciate ageing especially in contemporary urban settings. In discussing 'Place' as a development concept Tournier (1966) emphasizes the importance of appreciating where one is at a particular state of his/her development, affirming one's self and the place when one is there, and being prepared to leave the cherished place when it is time to do so. The truth about most human beings, however, is that they have regrets, being where they are, and anxiety about moving to the next place when it is time to do so. It is because of this that there is so much dread at the intimation of retirement and so little expression of joy among so many retirees.

For me, retirement is the 'place' from which one gets a view of one's life as an adventure and succession of opportunities to undertake and complete tasks with varying degrees of satisfaction to one's self.

Of course, the value of one's work to one depends a great deal upon the degree of approval expressed by others whom one considers significant and trustworthy. It is from the vantage point of retirement that one is able to view the future with all its unpredictability, with a sense of hope and patience, patience especially among the young, the fearful, the adventurous, and the pessimistic. As a retiree I consider myself a beneficiary not only of the goodness of God but also of the good will, the encouragement, and more than anything else, the forgiveness of hosts of persons in many spheres of reference during my comparatively long life. As a beneficiary of so much therefore, I have an obligation to be a generous contributor to the building of a better world in which more and more of my fellow humans stand in need of what contributes to the strengthening of hope and the overcoming of fear and fatalism.

In the final analysis, it is in retirement that one ought to become fully aware of what it is to be truly human. This is especially so with one who has been exposed to the teachings of someone like Jesus the Christ. Regrettably, in a country like Jamaica there are many retirees who are left without resources to provide themselves with the minimum for the sustenance of life above the poverty line. This is why persons should be advised to begin to prepare for retirement decades before they begin to receive a pension, rather than a salary or a stipend.

It is also important that persons acquire the discipline of being part of permanent personal relationships not only with families of origin and procreation but also with professional or occupational colleagues, platonic friends and next door neighbours. There is nothing more devastating to an older person than to have no one to call upon to share confidences with. Needless to say, both the value and discipline of friendship have to be learned and internalized throughout one's total lifespan. For me, it has been a great blessing to have access to the ears, hearts, and knowledge banks of a number of persons of varying age ranges, levels of intellectual sophistication, religious orientation and aesthetic interests. Thanks to many of my teachers and friends throughout my career I have learned to listen, appreciate humour and trust others so that now as an older person I can celebrate the experience of being able to share in rehearsing the nation's story for the benefit of those who need to hear aspects of it that they need to know, in order to find their own authentic place in the scheme of things.

Retirement has been for me, very active, very challenging, full of meaning, full of all sorts of blessings. I am extremely fortunate to be able to receive and savour these blessings. However, I must hasten to say that for this I owe a great deal to a number of persons and choices that I have been fortunate enough to make in circumstances which others helped to create. Without these persons and circumstances, like countless numbers of other retirees, I would have been full of regrets and recriminations.

I am thankful to my parents for instilling in me a number of core values. It was from them that I learned to make do with what I have at the present moment and make plans to achieve or earn for myself, what I think would be desirable in the future. It is from them and the elders in the local community in which I was cradled, that I learned that however difficult my own personal situation might be, there are those whose situations would be much more difficult than my own. It was also from them that I learned the spiritual value of sharing what I have with others and not losing an opportunity to help someone in need of the help.

I remain eternally grateful to my father who taught me the value of reading and instilled in me the habit of buying my own books in which I would be free to mark, re-read and to share with those who might be in need of what might be learned through these books.

The state of my mental and spiritual health would hardly be as it is had I not made the choice of courses I did when I did graduate work during the early to mid-nineteen sixties. My current world view and self-concept are sources of the sense of meaning which is an integral component of personal wellbeing and spiritual health. Courses designated 'Ideology, Man and History', taught by Professor Charles West, 'Theology and Personality' by Professors Seward Hiltner and James Emerson, have provided me with invaluable resources for continual renewal of my vision of the world and myself. It is out of my learning from these courses that I derive my interests in the subjects of Hope, Forgiveness, Shame, Psychology and History, Interfaith Dialogue et al. Fortunately for me, I have been provided with opportunities not only to write and make presentations to interested groups on issues related to these areas of concern, but also to teach undergraduate and postgraduate students continually. All of this has provided me with continual renewal which is further enhanced by the habit of walking for an hour around the Mona Dam which is the source of much of the potable water for the use of just under a million inhabitants of the Kingston Metropolitan area.

Having said all that I have said about mental, intellectual, physical and attitudinal preparations for later years, I hasten to add that life would be much less enjoyable and meaningful had I not been blessed with the family of procreation made up of my wife Winnifred, my daughters Faith and Grace, my son Bertrand, and more recently my daughter-in-law Sharon and grandchildren Hannah and Johnathan.

Among the many lessons I have learned about family is that if you want to derive maximum benefits from being husband, father, father-in-law or grandfather, you have to be prepared to give without counting the cost, to be continually mindful of the feelings of family members, to say as little as possible when you are angry, to remember dates and times that are important to family members, to complain as little as possible or not at all, if you can, and to make sure not to borrow from family members or forget to repay, if loans are made to you by family members.

Enjoyable retirement is not possible unless there is reasonable freedom from debt or worry about the means of paying the bills for the means of meeting basic needs and increasing cost of health care. Fortunately for me, because of the disciplined approach to spending by my wife and our children, I do not have to be unduly concerned about the means of paying the bills for basic needs. No member of the family is given to splurging and each stands ready to help anyone that may be in any need at any time.

It is because of all of what I have tried to explain in the foregoing paragraphs, that to date, retirement is for me an inevitable stage of one's personal pilgrimage which one needs to be prepared to deal with when it comes, and therefore, to prepare for without undue anxiety.

'Chosen' or 'Called' for Ministry

Despite all that I have been persuaded to believe about 'call' in respect of the decision to pursue full-time work in the Church as a pastor, pastoral administrator and preacher after over 50 years since I was approved by the former Presbyterian Church in Jamaica in 1949, I am still of the view that in my case, it was choice by God in collaboration with persons other than my parents or myself.

As mentioned elsewhere it was the wish of my nationalistic father that I pursue a career in law with the renowned J.A.G. Smith as my role model. The great jurist and legislator were not only black but also from the Parish of Hanover, not many miles from where my 'old man' grew up. Of course, without the usual basic educational foundation provided by the traditional grammar schools of the pre-Norman Manley era of Jamaican politics I would have to get into legal studies by the route of the matriculation examination made accessible to persons outside of Great Britain by the University of London. I planned to get there by way of teaching. So I taught at the Williamsfield Primary School in Westmoreland for three years during which time I had pupils such as Minister of Agriculture of the late 90's and early 2000's, Roger Clarke.

Something happened on the late afternoon of the annual agricultural show on the Frome Sugar estates' show grounds, 1948. As I was standing alone reflecting on some of the things I had seen during the day, the Rev. John Wint, my mother's pastor came along and engaged me in conversation about my future. Among the things he said to me was that he was aware that I was trying to make up my mind about what to do in life from there on. Before I could complete a sentence in response, with the typical John Wint smile on his face, he said "I have been observing you for a long time and praying for you. I am convinced that you are the type of young man we are looking for in the service of theChurch. Think about it and talk with me again when you think you need some help in making up our mind".

When I spoke to my father about what the Rev. Wint had said to me, his immediate response was: "I can't make up your mind for you but I can tell you that I would not be too happy about that. I am not so happy about some of those Ministers. However, give yourself about a year before you makeup your mind". Of course, at that time he was a deacon at the Baptist Church, the Minister of which was the Rev. Clarence Whylie whose church I attended most Sundays while I stayed in Williamsfield where I was teaching in the primary school.

When after a year I told my father that I was convinced that the Christian Ministry was where God wanted me to serve, his reply was that he would give me as much help as he could and would pray that I become a faithful man of God and not like some he had known.

Interestingly enough, during the years of my training he became a member of the Presbyterian Church in which he was made an elder and was even selected to represent the church at Synod dung the late fifties.

My call to ministry has been both challenged and tested ever since the afternoon when I was confronted by my mentor. The late great John Samuel Wint was to play a significant role in my formation as a theological student, pastor and leader in the Church. In many cases those who challenge, express disappointment that I did not follow a calling in which I might have been more directly involved in the struggle for political and social liberation. Students of the history of the Europeanisation of the Caribbean, insist that the so-called mainline Christian churches are instruments of colonial domination and by extension, a party to the suppression and depoliticisation of people of colour all over the world and especially in the Caribbean. Needless to say, I have lived with that conviction but long been convinced of the possibility of using my opportunities in the church of subverting these structures of domination. After nearly sixty years since I was asked to contemplate the possibility of serving God and the world in the capacity of a Christian Minister, I am fully assured that I did the right thing, and further, that like Jeremiah I was chosen by God before I made the choice in response to promptings by my mentor John Wint.

I have come to my conclusion about the appropriateness of my choice of vocation not only on the basis of what European and North America theologians have written about the Christian concept of call, but rather, on the basis of my own understanding of what is behind the word 'GOD' as used in our culture and the role of the prophet in Jewish and other traditions. I am convinced that despite my shortcomings and failings the purpose of my 'call' has been fulfilled in large measure in the course of my life, especially since the beginning of formal training for work as a servant-leader under the aegis of the Christian church.

Despite what would seem to many as my preoccupation with issues of ethnicity, and justice for blacks and other categories of victims of injustice in the name of church, state, class or gender, my call and the work that I have been privileged to do have reference not to any particular race, Christian tradition or religion, or nation, but indeed, to all of humankind. The practice of ministry has led me into interaction with fellow human beings of all continents and all social types. In the course of my ministry I have collaborated with Americans, Africans, Australians, Canadians, Chinese, Japanese, Koreans, Samoans, British (of England, Ireland, Wales and Scotland) and people of all language groups of the Caribbean. One of the discoveries that I have made is that in the final analysis, it is our humanity that matters most not our racial identity, nationality, religion, gender, medical condition or age. My interaction with my brothers and sisters of the various nationalities has led me to the conclusion that the call to service in any career is a call to work with God in what God is doing to set human beings and other areas of God's creation free to achieve maximum fulfillment in history. In short, as one called of God my obligation to the enslaved in Eastern Europe, India or North America is not less than the one to the oppressed in Southern or Western Africa and in the Caribbean. The context of enslavement may differ but the objective of efforts at liberation is the same in the light of my understanding of God and the mission of Christ to which my call is related. By the same token, it is my view that enslavement in the context of any form of religion is obstructive to the process of creation, as political, social, and economic enslavement, according to my own theology. Therefore there can be no distinction between what I do in Evangelism in the context of the church and what I do in politics in the context of my country of citizenship. I get this from my reading of the Jewish prophets and the record of life and the ministry of Jesus the Christ who lived his early life in the context of the political, religious and social milieu of a small town in the Middle East. My call was a call to minister in God's world in relation to every aspect of life in God's world. Needless to say, this call comes to every human being in some form or another and it is no less valid when it is not interpreted in relation to what, in my case, I refer to as the Christian Ministry. My father's call to farming and village leadership was no less valid than mine. So is my mother's call to mothering, my wife's call to teaching in the formal school system of the nation, and for that matter, the call of anyone else, to make his/her contribution to the making of the world. One of the regrettable things about the language of the institutionalized church is the tradition of assigning a higher value to the work of the 'ordained' person and using the words 'call' and 'calling' only of the vocation of the priest or Minister.

The traditional view of vocation within the Christian community and throughout the history of organized religion, has led not only to the undervaluing of the contribution of persons to the common good but also to the persistence among Christians of the view that those designated 'pastor', 'priest' or Minister in the Christian community should be only marginally involved in the cut and thrust of the life of the local community or nation. So many Christians view with suspicion the open involvement of religious leaders in elective politics.

They hold the view that one cannot be faithful to one's 'call' to preach and give pastoral leadership while being seriously involved in political leadership at any level. In the context of Jamaica this is rather interesting since so many of the pioneers in the making of the nation's political history have been leaders of the Christian church, lay and ordained. As many as three of those designated 'National Hero' were deacons of the pre- emancipation and immediate post-emancipation periods of the nation's history. Again, it is on record that among the founding members of one of our political parties were two ordained clergymen of the Anglican and Methodist churches.

In the tradition of the prophets of the Old Testament I have seen my own call to ministry as a challenge to give leadership to the community in its entirety and not just to the small segment of it referred to as 'church', 'denomination' or 'congregation'. The notion of the sovereignty of God over all creation is incompatible with that of a God whose concern is limited to 'spiritual' transformation of persons and with only that segment of humanity that is deemed to be the community of those referred to as "faithful".

In my own view, my call has reference to everyone and everything that falls under the sovereignty of God. This is why I feel no compunction about reaching out to all human beings, not just across Christian denominations, but indeed across all religious and ideological divides. Needless to say, this explains my commitment to ecumenical and interfaith relationships. It is also the reason I have always seen evangelization in terms of setting persons free to affirm the world which is the object of God's love and enabling those who are free to 'grow into the fullness of the stature of Christ', to become truly human in the sense in which creation of humankind is referred to in the first chapter of the book of Genesis. It is in this view that I speak without reservation, not only of theologies of liberation but also of theology as an instrument of liberation, the sense in which Jesus perceived it, as reported in the eighteenth verse of the second chapter of the Gospel according to Luke.

CPSIA information can be obtained
at www.ICGtesting.com
Printed in the USA
BVHW031122110719
553192BV00005B/37/P